The Cost of the Call

What It Means to Follow Christ

Diego Colón Batiz

© 2024 "The Cost of the Call" By: Diego Colón Batiz.
All rights reserved. Total or partial reproduction of this work by any means is prohibited without the proper authorization of the author.
ISBN: 979-8-9922869-3-9
Library of Congress Control Number: 2024927557
Copyright publication by 'Diego Colon Ministries'.
Tel: 407-900-1995
Email: pastor.diegocolon@gmail.com
Orlando, Florida, USA

Publisher: Baute Production
https://baute-production-publisher.tiiny.site
Tel: (813) 693-8879
Email: authors@usa.com
Tampa, Florida, USA. 2016.
Designs: Héctor Torres Gómez

Table of Contents

Preface 5

Introduction 7

Chapter 1: What Does the Calling Mean? 11

Chapter 2: Denying Oneself: The First Step 21

Chapter 3: Carrying the Cross: A Life of Surrender ... 29

Chapter 4: The Cost of Commitment 39

Chapter 5: The Sacrifice of Self-Will 49

Chapter 6: The Spiritual Warfare of the Disciple 59

Chapter 7: The Reward of the Call 67

Chapter 8: The Call to Serve: The Example of Christ 75

Chapter 9: Persecution and Rejection: The Path of the Disciple 83

Chapter 10: Forsaking All: The Testimony of the Apostles. 91

Chapter 11: Death to Self: Living for Christ 101

Chapter 12: The Call of Today: A Challenge to the Modern Church 109

Epilogue: A Call to Total Surrender 117

Questions for Deeper Insight 121

About the Author 127

Foreword

Obeying God's call is a journey filled with challenges, sacrifices, and difficult decisions—many of which seem illogical from a human perspective. Yet it is precisely in that apparent lack of logic that God shapes our character and reveals His eternal purpose. This book was born out of the conviction that the cost of the call is not a one-time payment but an ongoing process of surrender and trust in God's plan.

In my nearly 30 years of ministry, I have witnessed men and women respond to God's call with enthusiasm, only to face disappointments and trials that push them to the brink of doubt. I have walked that same path, questioning at times whether the sacrifices were worth it. Yet every step, even the most painful ones, has reaffirmed a vital truth: God's call is never easy, but it is always transformative.

The Scriptures are filled with examples of people who, in answering God's call, faced moments of uncertainty, rejection, and sacrifice. From Abraham leaving his homeland to Paul enduring prisons and shipwrecks, obedience has always come with a cost. This book seeks to connect those stories with our own lives, showing how God uses our circumstances, gifts, and weaknesses to fulfill His purpose.

We often think that obeying God is an act of faith that produces immediate results. However, the reality is that obedience frequently leads us to the wilderness, to isolation, or even to the misunderstanding of those around us. It is in those moments that we face the crucial question: Are we willing to follow Christ, even when the road is uncertain or painful?

"The Cost of the Call" is not intended to be an exhaustive guide or a manual of easy answers. Instead, it is a reflection on the depth of God's call and what it means to walk in radical obedience. My hope is that as you read these pages, you find comfort in God's promises and strength to face trials with faith and determination.

God is not looking for perfection; He is looking for willingness. He doesn't call the equipped; He equips the called. My prayer is that this book inspires you to embrace the cost of the call with courage, recognizing that every sacrifice is worth it when it is for the One who called us out of darkness into His marvelous light.

Introduction

A Call That Costs Everything

At the heart of every human being lies a longing for purpose. We search for something greater than ourselves, something that gives meaning to our lives. But the world we live in offers false promises of success and personal fulfillment at no cost. It teaches us that we can have it all, that comfort and happiness are within our reach if we just follow the right steps. However, Jesus shows us a radically different path. His call is not to comfort or earthly prosperity but to a life of surrender, sacrifice, and total obedience to God.

When Jesus called His first disciples, He did not promise them wealth or fame. Instead, He told them they must deny themselves, take up their cross, and follow Him (Luke 9:23). This call remains the same today. No matter how modern our society is or how different our challenges may be, the cost of following Christ remains unchanged. He has not softened His message to fit our times. On the contrary, He continues to invite us to leave everything behind for Him, to live for a Kingdom that is not of this world.

This book is born from the conviction that, in a world that values personal success and comfort so highly, true discipleship has been diluted. The church, in many cases, has adapted its message to the desires of modern culture, forgetting that following Christ involves a cost. But Jesus never offered an easy path. In fact, He warned us that there would be tribulations, that we would face persecution and rejection for His sake. So why do so many churches today preach a message that seems to focus on blessing rather than sacrifice?

In these pages, we will explore what it truly means to follow Christ. We will look at the lives of those who, throughout history, have been willing to pay the price. From the first apostles to modern-day martyrs, the cost of discipleship has always been high. But those who have paid it have found something far more valuable than any earthly reward: they have found a life full in Christ.

The purpose of this book is not merely to teach about the cost of the call but to challenge you to examine your own walk with God. Have you considered what it costs you to follow Jesus? Or have you fallen into the trap of seeking a comfortable life, free from challenges and sacrifices? These are questions we must continually ask ourselves, because discipleship is not a one-time decision; it is a daily choice. Every day, Jesus calls us to take up our cross and follow Him.

In a world that pushes us to seek instant gratification, Jesus' invitation seems radical. He calls us to deny our desires, to place His will above our own, and to trust that through sacrifice, we will find true life. This is not a life the world can understand, but it is the life Christ offers us. He not only calls us to believe in Him but to live as He lived: a life marked by obedience and sacrifice.

Throughout this book, we will dive deeper into what it means to give up our personal ambitions, our dreams, and even our relationships, if necessary, for the sake of God's

Kingdom. We will see how Jesus Himself modeled this life of surrender and how He calls us to do the same. This is an invitation to live in a countercultural way, to challenge the values of the world, and to embrace the Kingdom of God with all that we are.

Discipleship is not a life of comfort. It is a life of service, sacrificial love, and surrender. Sometimes, obedience to God will not make sense. It may lead us to places of suffering or ask us to give up what we value most. But in every act of obedience, we discover something deeper: the character of God, His faithfulness, and His sustaining grace. When we obey, even when we do not understand, we experience a deeper dimension of our relationship with Him.

This book also seeks to challenge the spiritual complacency that can settle into our lives. The Christian life is not a state of static comfort but a continual call to move forward, to grow, and to be transformed. Jesus calls us to walk by faith, not by sight, and that often means trusting in His plan even when we cannot see the end of the road. It is a call to depend on His grace, knowing that our strength is not enough, but that His power is made perfect in our weakness.

There will be moments when obedience seems unjust. We will see people who do not follow Christ prosper while we face difficulties. But this book will lead you to see life through the eternal lens of God's Kingdom. In His Kingdom, success is not measured by earthly standards. What matters is our faithfulness, and our willingness to follow Him despite the circumstances. The true reward of following Christ is not always seen in this life, but the eternal rewards far outweigh any temporary sacrifice.

If you are willing to consider the cost, this book will be a guide to help you discern what God is calling you to do. It is not a book of formulas or easy promises. It is a call to live a life of radical faith, unshakable obedience, and sacrifice. It is a challenge to let go of the things the world values and to cling to the only treasure that has eternal worth: Christ Himself.

My prayer is that through these pages, you will hear the gentle but clear call of Jesus to follow Him more closely. That His Spirit will speak to you as you consider the cost of following Him, and that you will find in Him the strength to walk this path. Discipleship costs, but it is a cost worth paying, for whoever loses their life for Christ will find it.

Chapter 1
What Does the Calling Mean?

Introduction

The calling of Christ to believers is one of the most transformative and challenging aspects of the Gospel. Throughout the Gospels, we see how Jesus extends His call to people from different backgrounds, contexts, and lifestyles. However, this call is not simply an invitation to salvation, but a lifelong commitment that involves sacrifice, obedience, and total surrender. Jesus does not call us to follow Him for temporary gain but to participate in His eternal mission, bringing the message of the Kingdom of God to the world. This calling is profound and radical, and throughout the history of the church, millions of people have responded to this invitation, facing challenges, persecution, and sacrifices for the cause of Christ.

The calling of Christ is both an open invitation to all and a demand for personal transformation. Those who respond to this call are invited to leave behind their own ambitions and live for God's purposes. But what does this calling really mean? How can we understand the depth of what it means to follow Jesus? In this chapter, we will explore three key aspects of Christ's call: first, the nature of the call to believers; second, the difference between being called and being chosen; and third, the invitation to follow Christ in the Gospels. These themes will help us deepen our understanding of what it means to be a true disciple of Jesus.

The Calling of Christ to Believers

The calling of Christ to believers is, above all, an invitation to leave behind the old life and begin a new life in Him. In **Mark 1:16-20**, Jesus calls Simon, Andrew, James, and John while they are fishing by the Sea of Galilee. He says to them, ***"Come, follow me, and I will send you out to fish for people."*** Immediately, they left their nets and followed Him. This calling was more than just an invitation to listen to a teaching; it was a demand for a new life, a life in which their identity and purpose would be defined by Christ. In this sense, the calling of Christ is transformative. It is not just about adding a new belief to our life, but about a radical transformation that changes the course of our existence.

The calling of Christ is also an invitation to participate in His mission. When Jesus called His disciples, He did not promise them an easy life or comfort, but He invited them to participate in the work of extending the Kingdom of God. In **Matthew 28:19-20**, Jesus gives the Great Commission: ***"Go and make disciples of all nations."*** The call of Christ always involves a mission greater than our own lives. It is not just about receiving blessings but about becoming a blessing to others. This means that the calling is not passive, but active. Believers are called to be agents of change, bringing the message of salvation to the world and making disciples in all nations.

Furthermore, the calling of Christ is universal. Jesus calls all those who are "weary and burdened" to come to Him and find rest (**Matthew 11:28**). No matter what our background, history, or condition, the call of Christ is available to everyone. However, although the call is universal, the response to that call is individual. Each person must decide if they are willing to leave behind what hinders them from following Christ and embrace His call with all their heart. In the Gospels, we see that not everyone who was called by Jesus responded in the same way. Some, like the first disciples, left everything to follow Him, while others, like the rich young man, walked away sad, unable to let go of what they valued most.

Responding to the call of Christ requires sacrifice. In **Luke 9:23**, Jesus said, ***"Whoever wants to be my disciple must deny themselves and take up their cross daily and follow me."*** This call to deny oneself and take up the cross is one of the most radical demands of Christian discipleship. It is not just about believing in Jesus but about following Him, even when it means facing suffering, rejection, or personal sacrifices. Throughout the history of the church, Christians have understood this call as an invitation to a life of total surrender. From the martyrs of the early church to modern missionaries, millions of believers have taken up their cross and followed Jesus, trusting that the eternal rewards far outweigh any temporary sacrifice.

The call of Christ also has a communal component. We are not called to follow Christ in isolation, but as part of a community of faith. In **1 Peter 2:9**, we are told that we are ***"a chosen people, a royal priesthood, a holy nation, God's***

special possession." The call of Christ unites us with other believers in a common mission: to declare the praises of Him who called us out of darkness into His wonderful light. This communal aspect of the calling is crucial, as it reminds us that we are not alone in our walk with Christ. We are part of a larger body, the church, and together we participate in the mission of God.

In summary, the call of Christ to believers is an invitation to a transformed life, a life of mission and service, a life of sacrifice and community. It is not just about a change in our beliefs but a change in our identity, purpose, and mission in the world. By responding to the call of Christ, we become His disciples, active participants in the work of the Kingdom of God, bringing the message of salvation to a world that desperately needs it.

Being Called vs. Being Chosen

One of the most important distinctions in the New Testament is the difference between being called and being chosen. In **Matthew 22:14**, Jesus says, ***"For many are called, but few are chosen."*** This statement raises an important question: What does it mean to be called? And what does it mean to be chosen? To understand this distinction, it is necessary to delve into the nature of God's call and our response to that call.

Being called, in biblical terms, is an open invitation from God to all humanity. In **2 Peter 3:9**, we read that God *"is not slow in keeping his promise, as some understand slowness. Instead he is patient with you, not wanting anyone to perish, but everyone to come to repentance."* This universal call is an expression of God's love and grace, inviting all who hear the Gospel to enter into a relationship with Him. However, being called is not the same as being chosen. While everyone is called, not everyone responds to God's call in a way that leads them to be part of the chosen. Election involves an active response of faith and obedience to God's call.

Being chosen, on the other hand, implies a deeper and more committed relationship with God. In John 15:16, Jesus says to His disciples, "You did not choose me, but I chose you." This election is not based on our merits or abilities but on God's sovereign grace. The chosen are those who have responded to God's call with a life of faith, obedience, and transformation. Election is not a passive status; it is an active reality that involves living according to God's purpose and mission in the world.

God's election is also deeply connected to His sovereignty and redemptive plan. In **Ephesians 1:4-5**, Paul writes, *"For He chose us in Him before the creation of the world to be holy and blameless in His sight. In love, He predestined us for adoption to sonship through Jesus Christ."* This divine election is not arbitrary but an integral part of God's plan to redeem the world. Those who are chosen by God are called to participate in His redemptive plan, living holy lives and sharing the message of salvation with others. Election, therefore, is not only a privilege but also a responsibility.

Additionally, God's election requires perseverance. In **2 Peter 1:10**, we are exhorted to *"make every effort to confirm your calling and election."* This means that those who have been called and chosen by God are called to persevere in the faith, to live lives of continuous obedience, and to actively participate in God's mission. It is not enough to have been called; we must live according to that call and demonstrate our election through our actions. Perseverance in faith is a distinctive mark of the chosen, and those who persevere to the end are those who have truly been called and chosen by God.

Being chosen by God also implies a life of holiness and transformation. In **1 Peter 1:15-16**, we are told, ***"Be holy in all you do; for it is written: 'Be holy, because I am holy.'"*** Election is not a license to live as we please but a call to live according to the character of God. The chosen are those who have been transformed by God's grace and who seek to reflect His holiness in their daily lives. Election, therefore, involves a life of holiness, obedience, and continuous transformation.

In conclusion, while all are called, only those who respond with faith and obedience are chosen. God's election is not a mere label but an active reality that involves a life of perseverance, holiness, and mission. The chosen are those who have been transformed by God's grace and who live according to His purpose and mission in the world. Responding to God's call is not enough; we must persevere in the faith and live lives that reflect our election and commitment to Christ.

The Invitation to Follow Christ in the Gospels

In the Gospels, we see that Jesus extends His invitation to follow Him to people from different backgrounds, but not everyone responds in the same way. The invitation of Christ is radical and challenging and requires a personal and transformative response. In **Matthew 16:24**, Jesus says, ***"Whoever wants to be my disciple must deny themselves and take up their cross and follow me."*** This invitation to follow Christ is not an easy task. It involves denying ourselves, taking up our cross, and following Him, even when that means facing sacrifices, difficulties, or rejection.

One of the clearest examples of Christ's invitation is the story of the rich young man in **Matthew 19:16-22**. This man, although sincere in his search for eternal life, was not willing to pay the price of following Christ. When Jesus asked him to sell everything he had and follow Him, he went away sad because "he had great wealth." This story illustrates the cost of discipleship. Following Christ is not an invitation to an easy or comfortable life; it is an invitation to a life of sacrifice and total surrender. The rich young man could not accept this invitation because he was not willing to give up what he valued most.

In contrast, the story of Zacchaeus in **Luke 19:1-10** shows us a positive response to Christ's invitation. Zacchaeus, a tax collector despised by his community, was desperately seeking to see Jesus. When Jesus called him, Zacchaeus responded with repentance and generosity, promising to return what he had stolen and give half of his possessions to the poor. This response reflects the transformative power of Christ's invitation. When a person responds with faith and obedience, their life is radically transformed. Zacchaeus went from being a selfish and corrupt man to being generous and just, all as a result of his encounter with Christ.

The invitation of Christ is also inclusive. Jesus did not only call the rich or the powerful but also those marginalized and rejected by society. In **John 4**, Jesus meets a Samaritan woman at the well in Sychar. This woman, who had lived a life of sin and rejection, was transformed by Christ's invitation. After hearing Jesus, she left her water jar and ran to her village to share the news of her encounter with the Messiah. Christ's invitation does not discriminate; He calls everyone, regardless of their past or social status, and offers them a new and transformed life.

In the Gospels, we also see that Christ's invitation is an invitation to faith and trust in Him. In **John 6:35**, Jesus says, *"I am the bread of life. Whoever comes to me will never go hungry, and whoever believes in me will never be thirsty."* Following Christ means depending completely on Him for our spiritual needs. It is an invitation to stop seeking satisfaction in the things of the world and to find our fulfillment in Christ. This invitation to faith is an invitation to a deep and ongoing relationship with Jesus, where we trust Him for every aspect of our life.

Finally, Christ's invitation is an invitation to mission. In the Gospels, we see that Jesus not only called people to follow Him but also sent them to share His message with others. In **Matthew 28:19-20**, Jesus gives the Great Commission: *"Go and make disciples of all nations."* This invitation to mission is an integral part of Christ's calling. Those who follow Jesus are not only called to receive but also to give. We are called to be His witnesses in the world, bringing the message of salvation to all we encounter.

In summary, Christ's invitation in the Gospels is radical, inclusive, and transformative. It is an invitation to a life of faith, sacrifice, and mission. Those who respond to this invitation experience a deep transformation in their lives and participate in Christ's mission in the world. Following Jesus is not easy, but it is the only path to the full and abundant life that He promises.

Conclusion

The call of Christ is more than just an invitation; it is a demand for total transformation. Throughout the Gospels, we see that Christ's call is an invitation to leave everything behind and follow Him with all that we are. It is not enough to hear the call; we must respond with a life of faith, obedience, and perseverance. Being called is not the same as being chosen; election involves a life committed to Christ and His mission. Those who respond to the call of Christ are transformed and empowered to participate in the work of the Kingdom of God.

Following Christ is not easy, but it is the only path to a full and meaningful life. Through Christ's call, we are invited to participate in His redemptive mission, bringing the message of salvation to a world that desperately needs it. By responding to this call, we discover that in Christ we find true life—a life of purpose, mission, and transformation. As believers, we are called to follow Christ with all that we are, trusting that through our surrender, we will experience the fullness of life that He promises.

Chapter 2

Denying Oneself: The First Step

Introduction

The call of Jesus to deny oneself is one of the most challenging principles of Christian discipleship. This mandate, presented in **Matthew 16:24** when Jesus declares, *"If anyone wants to come after me, let him deny himself, take up his cross, and follow me,"* is key to understanding what it means to be a true follower of Christ. Denying oneself goes against our human nature and the values of a society that teaches us to always seek the best for ourselves. However, for those who have decided to follow Christ, this denial is not merely an act of renunciation, but a step towards true freedom and the abundant life that Jesus promises.

Denying oneself is not a fleeting concept nor an optional suggestion; it is the first step on the path of discipleship. Without this denial, we cannot experience the life that Christ desires for us, a life in which He is the center, and our will is completely submitted to His. In this chapter, we will explore three fundamental aspects of this call to deny oneself: first, what it means to deny oneself according to **Matthew 16:24**; second, how modern culture contradicts this principle; and third, biblical testimonies of people who gave up everything to follow Christ.

Self-Denial in Matthew 16:24

In **Matthew 16:24**, Jesus presents one of the most radical statements of His ministry: ***"If anyone wants to come after me, let him deny himself, take up his cross, and follow me."*** This mandate challenges the expectations of Jesus' followers, who likely expected a Messiah who would liberate them from Roman rule and offer them a life of prosperity and power. Instead, Jesus speaks of the need to deny oneself and take up the cross, a symbol of death and suffering. This is the first step on the path of discipleship, and without it, we cannot truly follow Christ.

Denying oneself, in the context of **Matthew 16:24**, means renouncing our own ambitions, desires, and priorities. It is not just about avoiding certain sins or behaving morally, but about submitting our entire life and will to God's plans. It is a call to put Christ's interests above our own and to live for His glory instead of ours. This involves a willingness to sacrifice our comforts, dreams, and personal aspirations for the sake of God's Kingdom.

The expression "carrying his cross" in this verse adds an even deeper dimension to the concept of self-denial. In the time of Jesus, the cross was a symbol of death, and carrying a cross meant being on the way to execution. By asking us to take up our cross, Jesus calls us to be willing to die to ourselves, to our desires, and to our will. This act of taking up the cross is not an occasional sacrifice but a daily commitment. In **Luke 9:23**, Jesus adds that we must take up our cross "daily," indicating that self-denial is an ongoing process and not a one-time event.

Self-denial also implies a life of humility and service. Jesus is the supreme example of this attitude of self-denial. In **Philippians 2:5-8**, Paul describes how Jesus *"emptied himself, taking the form of a servant,"* and humbled himself to the point of death on the cross. If we want to follow Christ, we must adopt the same attitude of humility and service. This means we do not seek our own glory, but the glory of God. We do not seek to be served, but to serve others, just as Christ did.

Self-denial is also a form of worship. **Romans 12:1** exhorts us to *"present our bodies as a living sacrifice, holy and pleasing to God,"* which is our "reasonable worship." Denying oneself is an act of worship in which we offer all that we are to God as a sacrifice. This goes far beyond our outward actions; it is a total surrender of our being to God, allowing Him to work in us and through us for His purpose.

Finally, self-denial frees us from the chains of selfishness and materialism that often govern our lives. Instead of seeking our own satisfaction, we find our fulfillment in Christ. By dying to ourselves, we discover the true life that Jesus promised: *"For whoever wants to save his life will lose it; but whoever loses his life for my sake will find it"* (**Matthew 16:25**). This is the great mystery of the Gospel: by giving up our life, we find true life in Christ.

The Contradiction of Modern Culture

The call of Jesus to deny oneself completely contradicts the values of modern culture. We live in a society that promotes individualism, personal success, and instant gratification. From an early age, we are taught to "follow our dreams" and to "look out for number one." Social media, advertising, and the media constantly bombard us with the message that we must focus on our own happiness and well-being. However, the Gospel of Christ presents a completely opposite narrative.

Modern culture tells us that we must "follow our heart," but the Bible warns us that *"the heart is deceitful above all things"* (**Jeremiah 17:9**). The idea of following our own desires and emotions is dangerously misleading from a biblical perspective. Christ's call is to deny ourselves, which means we must not trust in our own desires but in God's will. While culture promotes self-sufficiency, the Gospel calls us to depend entirely on Christ and to seek His direction in everything we do.

Materialism is another aspect of modern culture that directly contradicts Christ's call. In a society that values the accumulation of wealth and possessions, Jesus calls us to let go of anything that hinders us from following Him. In **Matthew 19:21**, Jesus tells the rich young ruler, *"If you want to be perfect, go, sell what you have and give to the poor, and you will have treasure in heaven; and come, follow me."* The young man's response, walking away sorrowfully because he had great wealth, reflects the tension between the world's values and Christ's radical call. For many, attachment to material things is an obstacle that prevents them from fully following Jesus.

Additionally, modern culture teaches us to avoid suffering at all costs. The entertainment and wellness industry is designed to provide comfort and instant pleasure. However, Christ's call to take up our cross implies a willingness to suffer for His sake. In **1 Peter 4:1**, we are told, *"Since Christ* *suffered in his body, arm yourselves also with the same attitude."* Instead of avoiding suffering, Christ's followers are called to embrace it as part of their discipleship, knowing that through suffering we are conformed to the image of Christ.

The pursuit of self-sufficiency is another aspect of modern culture that conflicts with Christ's call. While the world values independence and the ability to solve our own problems, Jesus calls us to total dependence on God. In **John 15:5**, Jesus says, *"Apart from me, you can do nothing."* Self-denial involves recognizing our inability to live according to God's purposes on our own. We need His grace and power to live lives that glorify Christ. Instead of relying on our own strength, we are called to depend entirely on the Holy Spirit.

Finally, modern culture values instant gratification, while the Gospel calls us to patiently wait on the Lord. In a world where everything moves quickly and where needs and desires are expected to be satisfied immediately, Jesus calls us to a life of patience and waiting on His perfect timing. **James 1:3-4** reminds us that patience is a virtue that is developed through trials. By denying ourselves and waiting on God, we develop a deeper faith and greater dependence on His provision.

Biblical Testimonies of Total Surrender

The Bible is full of examples of men and women who understood what it means to deny oneself and follow Christ with all their hearts. One of the clearest examples is the Apostle Paul. In **Philippians 3:7-8**, Paul writes, *"But whatever were gains to me I now consider loss for the sake of Christ. What is more, I consider everything a loss because* *of the surpassing worth of knowing Christ Jesus my Lord."* Paul gave up everything—his status, reputation, and security—to follow Christ. For him, self-denial was not just a theoretical concept but a daily lived reality.

Another example of total surrender is Moses. Although he was raised in Pharaoh's court, with all the privileges that entailed, Moses chose to identify with God's people and suffer with them. In **Hebrews 11:24-26**, we are told that *"by faith Moses, when he had grown up, refused to be known as the son of Pharaoh's daughter."* Moses gave up the riches of Egypt because he knew there was a greater purpose for his life. This is a powerful example of how self-denial is not just about abandoning material things, but about embracing God's call, even when it involves suffering and sacrifice.

In the New Testament, we also see the life of Stephen, the first Christian martyr. In Acts 7, we see how Stephen preached boldly, without fear of the consequences, and was stoned for his testimony. Even in his final moments, Stephen demonstrated an attitude of surrender and compassion, praying for those who were killing him: *"Lord, do not hold this sin against them"* (**Acts 7:60**). Stephen's life reflects the true essence of self-denial: being willing to give everything, even life itself, for the cause of Christ.

The prophet Jeremiah is also an example of someone who lived a life of self-denial. Despite his youth and the difficulties he faced, Jeremiah accepted God's call to be His spokesman in the midst of a rebellious nation. Throughout his ministry, Jeremiah suffered persecution, rejection, and isolation, but he never strayed from God's call. In **Jeremiah**

20:9, he declares, *"But if I say, 'I will not mention him or speak any more in his name,' his word is in my heart like a fire, a fire shut up in my bones."* Jeremiah's life teaches us that self-denial often involves enduring suffering for the sake of God's Kingdom.

In the Old Testament, we also find the example of Abraham, who was called to leave his land and his family to follow God's plan. In **Genesis 12:1**, God tells Abraham, *"Go from your country, your people and your father's household to the land I will show you."* Abraham obeyed without knowing where he was going, trusting in God's promise. His life is a testimony of what it means to deny oneself and fully trust in God. Abraham was even willing to sacrifice his son Isaac, demonstrating an unshakable faith in God's purpose.

Finally, the greatest example of self-denial is Jesus Himself. In **Philippians 2:6-8**, we are told that Jesus, *"being in very nature God, did not consider equality with God something to be used to his own advantage; rather, he made himself nothing by taking the very nature of a servant, being made in human likeness."* Jesus humbled Himself to the point of dying on the cross for our sins. His life and death are the supreme example of what it means to deny oneself. If we want to follow Jesus, we must be willing to walk the same path of humility, service, and sacrifice.

Conclusion

Denying oneself is the first step on the path of discipleship. This call of Jesus in **Matthew 16:24** challenges our human nature and the values of modern culture, but it is essential to living a full life in Christ. Through self-denial, we are freed from the chains of selfishness, materialism, and self-sufficiency, and we are transformed into humble and faithful servants of God's Kingdom. Like Paul, Moses, Stephen, Jeremiah, Abraham, and Jesus, we are called to live lives of total surrender, trusting that the eternal reward far outweighs any temporary sacrifice.

Responding to Jesus' call to deny oneself is not easy, but it is the only path to the true life He promises. By embracing this call, we discover that by losing our life for Christ's sake, we find the abundant life that only He can offer. As disciples of Christ, we are called to live countercultural lives, following His example of humility, service, and sacrifice, while actively participating in the mission of extending His Kingdom on earth.

Chapter 3
Carrying the Cross: A Life of Surrender

Introduction

One of the most powerful symbols of Christianity is the cross, not only as a reminder of Jesus' sacrifice but also as a sign of the radical call He extends to all His followers. In **Matthew 16:24**, Jesus declares, *"If anyone desires to come after Me, let him deny himself, and take up his cross, and follow Me."* This mandate is central to the Christian life and should not be misunderstood as a mere symbolic act or a figurative expression. Jesus is calling His disciples to a life of sacrifice, where carrying the cross means being willing to face suffering, persecution, and to renounce the things the world values in favor of a life centered on Him.

Carrying the cross is not an occasional act but a daily commitment. In **Luke 9:23**, Jesus says we must take up our cross "daily," implying a constant surrender to the will of God. This principle of carrying the cross is the essence of a life of surrender, where every aspect of our existence is aligned with God's purposes. In this chapter, we will explore three aspects of what it means to carry the cross: first, the symbolism of the cross in the believer's life; second, the practical implications of "carrying the cross" in our daily lives; and third, biblical examples of individuals who lived out this principle.

The Symbolism of the Cross in Believer's Life

The cross, in Jesus' time, was a symbol of death and humiliation. It was the instrument used by the Romans to execute criminals in the most shameful way possible. When Jesus spoke of taking up the cross, His listeners understood that He was speaking of a willingness to suffer and die. In the Christian context, the cross symbolizes much more than a form of execution. It represents Jesus' ultimate sacrifice for our sins, but it is also a call for each of us to die to ourselves in order to live for God. This call to take up our cross is, in essence, a call to renounce our former life to embrace a new life in Christ.

Carrying the cross also symbolizes total submission to God's will. In **Philippians 2:8**, we are told that Jesus *"humbled Himself and became obedient to the point of death, even the death of the cross."* When we take up our cross, we imitate the attitude of Christ, who fully surrendered to the Father's plan. In our lives, this means that we must be willing to relinquish our own plans and desires in order to follow the path God has laid out for us. This act of surrender is not a sign of weakness, but of total trust in God's wisdom and love.

The symbolism of the cross also involves suffering and persecution. In **John 15:20**, Jesus warns His disciples, *"If they persecuted Me, they will also persecute you."* Carrying the cross is not an invitation to a life of comfort and earthly success, but rather a preparation to face opposition and hardships for the sake of Christ. Christians throughout history have understood that following Jesus often means being rejected by the world. The cross then becomes a reminder that, although we face temporary suffering, our lives are rooted in eternal hope.

Additionally, the cross symbolizes the rejection of sin. In **Romans 6:6**, Paul writes, *"knowing this, that our old man was crucified with Him, that the body of sin might be done away with, that we should no longer be slaves of sin."* Taking up our cross means that we have died to the power of sin in our lives. We are no longer enslaved by our sinful desires, but we live in the freedom Christ has given us. This doesn't mean we won't face temptation, but it does mean that through the cross, we have the power to resist sin and live in holiness.

The act of carrying the cross is also an act of identity. By taking up our cross, we identify with Christ in His death and resurrection. In **Galatians 2:20**, Paul writes, *"I have been crucified with Christ; it is no longer I who live, but Christ lives in me."* This act of identification with Christ means that our life is no longer our own. We have been bought with a price, and we now live for the glory of God. The cross, therefore, is not only a symbol of sacrifice but a reminder of our new identity in Christ as children of God and heirs of His Kingdom.

Finally, the cross teaches us that victory comes through sacrifice. In the world, victory is often associated with strength, power, and success. But in the Gospel, Christ's victory over sin and death came through His sacrifice on the cross. Similarly, when we take up our cross and renounce our lives for the sake of Christ, we find true spiritual victory. In **Matthew 16:25**, Jesus says, *"For whoever desires to save his life will lose it, but whoever loses his life for My sake will* *find it."* This is the paradox of the Gospel: by dying to ourselves, we find true life in Christ.

The Practical Implications of "Carrying the Cross" in Our Daily Lives

Carrying the cross is not just a theological concept, but a practical reality that affects every aspect of our daily lives. Often, we think of carrying the cross as something reserved for extreme situations, but the truth is, we are called to carry our cross daily in the smallest decisions and actions of life. Jesus didn't say to take up our cross only in times of crisis, but "daily" (**Luke 9:23**). This implies that discipleship and a life of surrender are part of our daily routine, affecting how we live, think, and act.

One of the clearest ways we carry our cross daily is through our relationships with others. In **Philippians 2:3-4**, we are told, *"Let nothing be done through selfish ambition or conceit, but in lowliness of mind let each esteem others better than himself. Let each of you look out not only for his own interests, but also for the interests of others."* Carrying the cross means that we renounce our selfishness and pride and, instead, place the interests of others above our own. This can be difficult, especially in a culture that values individualism and self-indulgence, but it is a crucial aspect of Christian discipleship.

Carrying the cross also affects our priorities and how we manage our time and resources. Jesus calls us to seek first the Kingdom of God (**Matthew 6:33**), which implies that everything we do must be aligned with His purposes. This means that our decisions on how we use our money, our time, and our abilities should reflect our commitment to Christ. Often, this involves renouncing our own desires and comforts in order to serve others and advance the Kingdom of God. Carrying the cross is an invitation to a life of sacrifice where our priorities are in tune with the values of the Gospel.

Another practical implication of carrying the cross is the willingness to suffer for the Gospel. In **2 Timothy 3:12**, Paul warns, ***"Yes, and all who desire to live godly in Christ Jesus will suffer persecution."*** While not all Christians face physical persecution, we are all called to endure hardships for the sake of our faith. This may take the form of rejection, isolation, or mockery in our social circles, workplaces, or even within our own families. Carrying the cross means being willing to endure these trials, knowing that our suffering is not in vain but produces perseverance and character (**Romans 5:3-4**).

Furthermore, carrying the cross involves living a life of integrity and holiness in a world that often promotes sin and immorality. In **1 Peter 1:15-16**, we are told, ***"but as He who called you is holy, you also be holy in all your conduct, because it is written, 'Be holy, for I am holy.'"*** Carrying the cross means that we are committed to living according to God's standards, not the world's. This may require renouncing behaviors, habits, or relationships that do not glorify God. It is a call to purity, both in our actions and in our thoughts and motivations.

Carrying the cross also calls us to live in humility. In a world that values self-sufficiency and personal success, Jesus calls us to live humbly, recognizing that everything we have comes from God. In **James 4:10**, we are exhorted, ***"Humble*** *yourselves in the sight of the Lord, and He will lift you up."* Humility is not just an internal attitude but is reflected in our daily actions. Carrying the cross means that we acknowledge our constant need for God's grace and rely completely on Him for our strength and direction.

Finally, carrying the cross means living from an eternal perspective. Rather than focusing on the temporary things of this world, we carry our cross with our eyes set on the eternal rewards God has promised. In *2 Corinthians 4:17-18*, Paul writes, *"For our light affliction, which is but for a moment, is working for us a far more exceeding and eternal weight of glory, while we do not look at the things which are seen, but at the things which are not seen."* As we carry our cross, we remember that our current suffering is temporary and that the glory awaiting us in Christ far surpasses anything this world can offer.

Examples of People Who Lived Out This Principle

Throughout the Bible, we find numerous examples of individuals who lived out the principle of carrying their cross and surrendering everything to follow God. One of the most notable examples is the apostle Peter. After having denied Jesus three times, Peter was restored by Christ and spent the rest of his life preaching the Gospel. In **Acts 4:19-20**, we see Peter's courage when, alongside John, he was arrested for preaching in the name of Jesus. Despite threats from the authorities, Peter responded, *"Whether it is right in the sight of God to listen to you more than to God, you judge. For we cannot but speak the things which we have seen and heard."*

Peter understood that carrying his cross meant being willing to suffer persecution.

Another powerful example is Paul, who renounced his status and privileges as a Pharisee to follow Christ. In **Philippians 3:7-8**, Paul writes, *"But what things were gain to me, these I have counted loss for Christ. Yet indeed I also count all things loss for the excellence of the knowledge of Christ Jesus my Lord."* Paul lived a life of total surrender, traveling throughout the Roman Empire to preach the Gospel, facing imprisonments, beatings, and shipwrecks. Throughout his ministry, Paul experienced the cost of carrying his cross but also understood that eternal rewards far outweighed any earthly suffering.

In the Old Testament, we find the story of Abraham, who was called to sacrifice his son Isaac as a test of his faith. In **Genesis 22**, we see how Abraham, in obedience to God, was willing to give up what he loved most. Although God stopped Abraham from sacrificing Isaac, his willingness to obey illustrates what it means to carry the cross. Abraham was willing to trust God, even when the command seemed contrary to his own hopes and desires. This act of faith and obedience is a powerful example of what it means to surrender everything to follow God.

Another example from the New Testament is Stephen, the first Christian martyr. In **Acts 7**, we see how Stephen boldly preached about Christ, knowing that it would cost him his life. As he was being stoned, Stephen prayed, *"Lord, do not charge them with this sin"* (**Acts 7:60**). His willingness to die for his faith and his attitude of forgiveness toward his executioners are extraordinary examples of what it means to carry the cross. Stephen understood that following Christ meant being willing to surrender even his life for the sake of the Gospel.

Jeremiah is a powerful biblical example of what it means to carry one's cross and live a life of surrender. Known as the "weeping prophet," Jeremiah's ministry was marked by deep personal suffering, rejection, and persecution. He was mocked, beaten, and thrown into a cistern for proclaiming the message God gave him. Yet, despite the immense hardship, Jeremiah remained faithful to his calling. In **Jeremiah 20:9**, he confesses that even when he wanted to stop speaking God's words, they were like a fire in his bones, and he could not hold them in. His life exemplifies the cost of obedience to God, showing us that carrying the cross often involves enduring pain and rejection for the sake of His will.

Finally, Jesus Himself is the ultimate example of what it means to carry the cross. In **Hebrews 12:2**, we are told that Jesus, *"for the joy that was set before Him endured the cross, despising the shame."* Jesus not only called us to carry our crosses; He carried the cross for us, enduring suffering and death so that we might have eternal life. His sacrifice is the model we are to follow, knowing that, although the way of the cross is difficult, it is the only path that leads to true life.

Conclusion

Carrying the cross is not simply a metaphor; it is a call to a life of surrender, sacrifice, and total devotion to Christ. Through the cross, we learn that true victory and purpose are not found in seeking comfort or worldly success, but in being willing to give up everything to follow Christ. From the symbolism of the cross to the practical implications of carrying it daily, we are called to live lives that reflect the sacrifice of Jesus and the transforming power of His resurrection.

Following Christ is not an easy path, but it is the only one that leads to eternal life. Through biblical examples and the history of the church, we see that those who have faithfully carried their cross have experienced God's glory in profound ways. As disciples of Jesus, we are called to take up our cross daily, trusting that, although the road is difficult, the eternal rewards far surpass any temporary sacrifice. By carrying our cross, we find true life and eternal purpose in Christ.

Chapter 4

The Cost of Commitment

Introduction

One of the most important aspects of Christian discipleship is total commitment to Christ. The call to follow Jesus is not something that can be taken lightly or approached superficially. Jesus made it clear on several occasions that the cost of following Him is high and involves renunciations, sacrifices, and complete surrender. In **Luke 14:27-28**, Jesus said, ***"And whoever does not bear his cross and come after Me cannot be My disciple. For which of you, intending to build a tower, does not sit down first and count the cost, whether he has enough to finish it?"*** With these words, Jesus teaches us that following Him requires serious and thoughtful commitment.

The cost of commitment to Christ is a topic that is often not discussed enough in modern churches. We live in a culture that values comfort, quick success, and immediate rewards. However, the Gospel of Christ calls us to something much deeper: a life completely surrendered to His cause, even when that means losing the things the world considers valuable. In this chapter, we will explore three aspects of the cost of commitment: first, the price of following Christ in a world that stands against His principles; second, the stories of martyrs and Christians who have paid with their lives or possessions for following Christ; and third, how we can remain faithful under pressure in our lives today.

The Price of Following Christ in a World Against Him

Following Christ in a world that stands against His principles is not an easy task. From the beginning of Jesus' ministry, it became clear that the Kingdom of God challenges the values of the world. In **John 15:18-19**, Jesus warned His disciples, *"If the world hates you, you know that it hated Me before it hated you. If you were of the world, the world would love its own. Yet because you are not of the world, but I chose you out of the world, therefore the world hates you."* As Christians, we are called to live counterculturally, rejecting the temptations to conform to the patterns of this world. This inevitably leads us to face opposition, rejection, and, in some cases, persecution.

The price of following Christ in a world that opposes Him can manifest in many ways. On a personal level, it may mean losing friendships or relationships because of our convictions and lifestyle. On a social level, it may mean facing ridicule, criticism, or discrimination because of our faith. In more extreme contexts, following Christ can lead to direct persecution, such as imprisonment or even death. In **2 Timothy 3:12**, Paul warns, *"Yes, and all who desire to live godly in Christ Jesus will suffer persecution."* Christian discipleship is not an easy path; it is a call to face difficulties for the sake of the Gospel.

The price of commitment also includes the need to renounce the values and desires of this world. In **Matthew 6:19-20**, Jesus teaches, *"Do not lay up for yourselves* *treasures on earth, where moth and rust destroy and where thieves break in and steal; but lay up for yourselves treasures in heaven."* As followers of Christ, we are called to invest our lives in the eternal, rather than seeking the temporary gratification that this world offers. This may mean sacrificing our personal ambitions, desires for success, and comforts, knowing that the eternal rewards are infinitely greater than anything we can gain in this life.

In some cases, following Christ in a world that opposes Him means being willing to endure misunderstanding and even hatred from those who do not understand our commitment to God's Kingdom. In **Matthew 10:22**, Jesus said, *"And you will be hated by all for My name's sake."* This is a reminder that the Gospel of Christ, although a message of love and hope, is often rejected by those unwilling to submit to God's authority. As believers, we must be prepared to face this opposition with patience, humility, and perseverance, trusting that God will sustain us through the trials.

Another aspect of the cost of following Christ in a world against Him is the renunciation of our own wills and desires. In **Mark 8:34**, Jesus said, *"Whoever desires to come after Me, let him deny himself, and take up his cross, and follow Me."* This is a call to die to our own self, to our selfish ambitions, and to live for Christ. This does not mean we have no desires or personal goals, but it does mean that our lives are completely surrendered to God's will. The cost of commitment is, essentially, the total surrender of our being to Christ, allowing Him to be Lord over every aspect of our lives.

Finally, the price of following Christ in a world that is against Him includes the willingness to be witnesses of the Gospel, even when that involves personal risks. In **Acts 1:8**, Jesus said, *"But you shall receive power when the Holy Spirit has come upon you, and you shall be witnesses to Me in Jerusalem, and in all Judea and Samaria, and to the end of the earth."* Being witnesses of Christ is not an easy task, especially in a world that opposes the message of the Gospel. However, we are called to be lights in the darkness, proclaiming the truth of Christ with boldness and faithfulness, knowing that our testimony can have an eternal impact on the lives of those around us.

Stories of Martyrs and Christians Who Paid the Price

Throughout the history of the church, countless Christians have paid the ultimate price for following Christ. These martyrs and faithful witnesses are powerful examples of what it means to be committed to the Gospel to the very end. A notable martyr is Richard Wurmbrand, a Romanian Lutheran pastor who was arrested and imprisoned for his faith under the communist regime in Romania. Wurmbrand was brutally tortured for 14 years for preaching the Gospel and refusing to renounce Christ. Despite the physical and emotional suffering, he endured, Wurmbrand remained steadfast in his faith, testifying to his captors and fellow prisoners about the love and grace of God. His life is a powerful modern-day example of what it means to pay the price of commitment to Christ in a hostile world. His testimony has inspired millions of people around the world to persevere in the face of persecution.

In more recent times, during World War II, pastor and theologian Dietrich Bonhoeffer stood out as a brave witness of the Gospel. Bonhoeffer was a fierce opponent of the Nazi regime and advocated for active resistance against tyranny. He was arrested and eventually executed for his participation in a conspiracy to overthrow Hitler. In his book *The Cost of Discipleship,* Bonhoeffer wrote, **"When Christ calls a man, he bids him come and die."** His life and death are a reminder of the high cost of following Christ in a world that is against His principles.

The story of Jim Elliot is another modern and profound example of the cost of commitment to Christ. Elliot, along with four other missionaries, traveled to Ecuador to share the Gospel with the Huaorani tribe, a group known for its violence and isolation. Despite the risks, Elliot believed that God's call was worth any sacrifice. In 1956, he and his companions were killed by the very people they sought to reach. Elliot's famous words, **"He is no fool who gives what he cannot keep to gain what he cannot lose,"** encapsulate his deep understanding of eternal priorities. His life and death continue to inspire countless believers to give their all for the Gospel, reminding us that true commitment often requires the ultimate sacrifice.

Christian martyrs are not just figures from the past; in many places around the world today, believers continue to pay the price for their faith. In countries where Christianity is illegal or heavily persecuted, thousands of Christians face daily threats of imprisonment, torture, and even execution. However, these believers remain faithful to Christ, knowing that *"if we endure, we shall also reign with Him"* **(2 Timothy 2:12).** Their stories challenge us to consider whether we are willing to pay the same price for our faith, knowing that eternal rewards far surpass any temporary suffering.

In many cases, Christians who have paid the price for their faith have done so not only with their lives but also with their possessions and social status. In **Hebrews 10:34**, we are told that the early Christians ***"joyfully accepted the plundering of your goods, knowing that you have a better and an enduring possession for yourselves in heaven."*** These believers understood that the material things of this world are temporary, and they were willing to give up everything for the cause of Christ. Their example challenges us to evaluate our own priorities and consider whether we are willing to surrender our comforts and possessions for the Kingdom of God.

Finally, the martyrs and faithful witnesses show us that the cost of commitment is not something to be feared, but something to be embraced with joy. In **Acts 5:41**, after being beaten for preaching Christ, the apostles ***"departed from the presence of the council, rejoicing that they were counted worthy to suffer shame for His name."*** The joy of suffering for Christ is a mystery that only those who have experienced the depth of His love can understand. These martyrs and faithful witnesses inspire us to live with the same willingness to suffer, knowing that, in the end, our reward is in heaven.

How to Stay Faithful Under Pressure

One of the most important questions we face as Christians is how to remain faithful under pressure. In a world that opposes the principles of the Gospel, it is easy to give in to the temptation to conform to society's expectations or compromise our faith to avoid rejection or persecution. However, Jesus calls us to persevere until the end. In **Matthew 24:13**, Jesus said, *"But he who endures to the end shall be saved."* Faithfulness in the midst of trials is not optional for the believer; it is a distinguishing mark of those who truly follow Christ.

One of the keys to staying faithful under pressure is maintaining a constant life of prayer. In **Matthew 26:41**, Jesus warned His disciples, *"Watch and pray, lest you enter into temptation."* Prayer not only strengthens us spiritually but also helps us stay focused on God, even when we face trials. Through prayer, we renew our dependence on God and find the strength needed to persevere. Christians who have remained faithful in the midst of persecution have often been people of deep prayer, trusting that God would sustain them in their darkest moments.

Another way to remain faithful under pressure is to remember God's promises. In **John 16:33**, Jesus said, *"In the world you will have tribulation; but be of good cheer, I have overcome the world."* This promise assures us that although we face difficulties and opposition, Christ has already triumphed over sin, death, and the forces of evil. Keeping our eyes on God's promises gives us hope and strength to press on, knowing that our trials are temporary and that the final victory is assured in Christ.

Christian community is also essential to remaining faithful under pressure. In **Hebrews 10:24-25**, we are exhorted to *"consider one another in order to stir up love and good works, not forsaking the assembling of ourselves together, as is the manner of some, but exhorting one* *another."* The Christian life was not designed to be lived in isolation. When we face pressure or persecution, it is vital that we lean on the community of faith. Through fellowship with other believers, we find encouragement, support, and strength to persevere. The church is a refuge in the storm, and it is there that we can be built up and strengthened in our faith.

Remaining faithful under pressure also requires absolute trust in God's sovereignty. In **Romans 8:28**, we are assured that *"all things work together for good to those who love God."* This promise reminds us that even when we face trials, God is working for our good and for His glory. Trusting in God's sovereignty gives us the peace and security that, although we may not always understand why things happen, we can trust that God is in control and that He is working according to His perfect plan.

Finally, a keyway to remain faithful under pressure is to have an eternal perspective. In **Colossians 3:1-2**, we are exhorted to *"seek those things which are above, where Christ is, sitting at the right hand of God. Set your mind on things above, not on things on the earth."* When we face difficulties, it is easy to focus on the immediate problems, but Jesus calls us to have an eternal perspective. We know that this world is temporary and that our true reward is in heaven. By keeping our eyes on Christ and the eternal rewards, we can endure any trial, knowing that what awaits us in eternity far surpasses any temporary suffering.

Conclusion

The cost of commitment to Christ is high, but the eternal rewards far exceed any sacrifice we may make in this life. Throughout history, faithful Christians have paid with their lives, possessions, and social status for following Jesus, and their testimonies inspire us to live with the same willingness to suffer for the sake of the Gospel. In a world that opposes the principles of Christ, we are called to remain faithful, knowing that although we face trials and persecutions, our reward is in heaven.

Following Christ is not easy, but it is the only path that leads to eternal life. As we face the challenges and pressures of this world, we must remember that commitment to Christ requires perseverance, prayer, community, and an eternal perspective. By living according to these principles, we can stand firm in our faith, trusting that God will sustain us and reward us for our faithfulness. The cost of commitment is high, but the joy of following Christ is infinitely greater.

Chapter 5

The Sacrifice of Self-Will

Introduction

The sacrifice of self-will is one of the most profound challenges that any believer faces in their walk with Christ. Often, our decisions and desires are influenced by our emotions, personal interests, and the pressures of the world. However, following Christ means surrendering our will, submitting our decisions and desires to the Lordship of Jesus. This process of surrender is not easy, as it involves an internal struggle between what we want and what God wants for our lives. In **Matthew 26:39**, Jesus, in the Garden of Gethsemane, prayed, saying, *"My Father, if it is possible, may this cup be taken from me. Yet not as I will, but as you will."* This prayer of Jesus is a powerful example of what it means to sacrifice our self-will and submit it to God's will.

The sacrifice of self-will is not a decision that is made once, but a continuous process that defines the Christian life. In every circumstance, big or small, we are called to ask ourselves if our actions and desires align with God's purposes. In this chapter, we will explore three key aspects of what it means to sacrifice self-will: first, how to learn to submit our will to God's; second, the internal struggle of Jesus in Gethsemane as the supreme example of surrender; and third, the stories of people who gave up their own plans to follow God's will.

How to Learn to Submit Our Will to God's

Submitting our will to God's is an act of humility and obedience that requires a deep transformation of our hearts. Most of us are accustomed to making decisions based on what seems right to us or what benefits us the most. However, when we decide to follow Christ, we are asked to stop relying on our own understanding and, instead, fully trust in God's direction. **Proverbs 3:5-6** urges us, *"Trust in the Lord with all your heart and lean not on your own understanding; in all your ways submit to him, and he will make your paths straight."* This passage reminds us that our will must be subordinated to God's wisdom and plan.

The first step in learning to submit our will is recognizing that God knows what is best for our lives, even when we don't fully understand it. **Romans 12:2** tells us, *"Do not conform to the pattern of this world, but be transformed by the renewing of your mind. Then you will be able to test and approve what God's will is—his good, pleasing, and perfect will."* As we allow the Holy Spirit to transform our thinking, we begin to see the world and our decisions from God's perspective. Learning to submit our will involves allowing God to transform our hearts and minds so that our decisions reflect His plan and not our preferences.

Another important step in submitting our will is prayer. Prayer is the means by which we align ourselves with God's purposes and seek His guidance in our decisions. Jesus taught us to pray in the Lord's Prayer, *"Your will be done, on earth as it is in heaven"* **(Matthew 6:10).** This is a reminder that our will must always be subject to God's will. Through prayer, we not only present our requests to God, but we also seek His direction and strength to do what He desires. Prayer is a powerful tool for surrendering to God's will and discerning His purpose in our lives.

Submitting our will to God also requires faith. Often, God calls us to do things that don't make sense from a human perspective or that seem challenging. In **Hebrews 11:8**, we read about the faith of Abraham, who obeyed God's call to go to a place he did not know, fully trusting in God's promise. This active faith is essential to submitting our will to God because we often will not be able to see the outcome of our decisions immediately. However, we trust that God is working for our good and for His glory. Faith gives us the ability to move forward confidently, even when we don't fully understand God's plan.

The sacrifice of self-will also means being willing to give up our own desires and goals when they don't align with God's plan. In **Luke 9:23**, Jesus says, *"Whoever wants to be my disciple must deny themselves and take up their cross daily and follow me."* This call to deny ourselves is an invitation to surrender our lives and desires to God, trusting that His plans are better than ours. Denying ourselves is an act of daily surrender, where we decide that God's will takes priority over our own ambitions.

Finally, submitting our will to God leads to experiencing a deep and lasting peace. **Philippians 4:6-7** encourages us to present our requests to God with thanksgiving, and promises that *"the peace of God, which* *transcends all understanding, will guard your hearts and your minds in Christ Jesus."* When we surrender our will to God, we stop fighting for control of our lives and rest in the certainty that He is in control. This peace comes from trusting that by following God's will, we are walking the best path, even when we face challenges.

The Internal Struggle of Jesus in Gethsemane as the Supreme Example

The most intense moment of Jesus' surrender of His own will occurred in the Garden of Gethsemane. This episode, narrated in **Matthew 26:36-46**, gives us an intimate view of the internal struggle Jesus faced as He prepared for the ultimate sacrifice on the cross. Jesus knew what awaited Him: betrayal, physical suffering, rejection, and death. But more than that, He knew He would carry the weight of the world's sin. In this moment of anguish, Jesus prayed three times to the Father, saying, *"My Father, if it is possible, may this cup be taken from me. Yet not as I will, but as you will"* (**Matthew 26:39**).

This passage shows Jesus' humanity and the depth of His internal struggle. Though He was God, Jesus experienced the pain and anxiety that comes with surrendering one's will. Yet in the midst of His anguish, He chose to fully submit to the Father's will. This is the supreme example of what it means to sacrifice self-will. Through His surrender, Jesus teaches us that obedience to God's will is the path to fulfilling the divine purpose, even if it involves suffering and sacrifice.

Jesus' prayer in Gethsemane also shows us that surrender is not always easy or immediate. Jesus prayed repeatedly, asking for the cup to pass from Him if possible. This shows us that we should not feel guilty for struggling with God's will in our lives. Sometimes, obedience can be painful and difficult, but what matters is that, in the end, we choose to submit to God. Jesus, in His humanity, faced the same struggle that we face when our desires do not align with God's.

Jesus' surrender in Gethsemane was also an act of love. He was willing to sacrifice His own will and suffer for the sake of humanity. In **John 15:13**, Jesus said, *"Greater love has no one than this: to lay down one's life for one's friends."* Jesus' surrender was not just mechanical obedience, but an act of love toward the Father and us. Similarly, when we surrender our will to God, we do so not out of obligation, but out of love for the One who loved us first. Love drives us to trust that God's will is better and that by following His path, we reflect Christ's love in our lives.

Another aspect of Jesus' struggle in Gethsemane is the importance of spiritual strength in times of trial. In **Luke 22:43**, we are told that *"an angel from heaven appeared to him and strengthened him."* Despite the intensity of the internal struggle, God sent His help at the moment of greatest need. Similarly, when we face the difficult task of surrendering our will, we can trust that God will strengthen us through the Holy Spirit. Spiritual strength does not eliminate the struggle but enables us to persevere in obedience, even when it seems like we cannot go on.

Finally, Gethsemane teaches us that surrendering to God's will is the path to victory. Although Jesus' sacrifice on the cross seemed like a defeat from a human perspective, it was, in fact, the greatest act of spiritual victory in history. Through His obedience, Jesus defeated sin, death, and the power of the enemy. In the same way, when we sacrifice our will and follow God's will, even though it may seem like we are losing, we are walking toward the victory that God has prepared for us. True victory in the Christian life is not found in getting what we want but in doing what God desires.

Stories of People Who Gave Up Their Plans to Follow God

Throughout biblical and church history, we find examples of people who were willing to give up their own plans and desires to follow God's will. One of the most powerful examples is Abraham. In **Genesis 12**, God called Abraham to leave his land and his family to go to a place he did not know. Abraham, despite not knowing where this call would take him, obeyed in faith. His willingness to sacrifice his comfort, security, and personal future to follow God is a clear example of what it means to surrender self-will. Later, Abraham was called to sacrifice his son, Isaac, once again demonstrating his complete trust in God's plans.

Another biblical example of surrender is Moses. Raised in the opulence of Pharaoh's court, Moses could have lived a comfortable and successful life. However, he chose to obey God's call to deliver the Israelites from slavery in Egypt. In **Hebrews 11:24-25**, we are told that *"Moses, when he had grown up, refused to be known as the son of Pharaoh's daughter. He chose to be mistreated along with the people of*

God rather than to enjoy the fleeting pleasures of sin." Moses sacrificed his status and privileges in Egypt to obey God's will and fulfill his divine purpose.

In the New Testament, the apostle Paul is a clear example of someone who gave up his own plans to follow God. Before his conversion, Paul (Saul) was a Pharisee who persecuted Christians. He had a promising career in Judaism and was committed to his mission of eradicating Christianity. However, when Jesus met him on the road to Damascus, Paul gave up his old life and became a fervent preacher of the Gospel. In **Philippians 3:7-8**, Paul wrote, *"But whatever were gains to me I now consider loss for the sake of Christ."* Paul sacrificed his reputation, his achievements, and his security to follow God's call.

A modern-day example of someone who gave up his own plans to follow God is William Carey, often called the "father of modern missions." Carey felt called by God to take the Gospel to India at a time when very few Europeans were willing to venture abroad to share their faith. Despite facing enormous obstacles, including poverty, illness, and the loss of loved ones, Carey persevered in his mission. He spent decades translating the Bible into several Indian languages and dialects and founded educational institutions that continue to impact the region today. His willingness to sacrifice his comfort and personal well-being to fulfill God's call is a clear example of what it means to surrender self-will to follow God's plans. His legacy continues to inspire missionaries and believers around the world.

Another contemporary example is Corrie ten Boom, a Dutch Christian who, during World War II, decided to hide persecuted Jews from the Nazis. Corrie and her family sacrificed their safety to save others' lives. Although she was arrested and sent to a concentration camp, where she suffered immensely, Corrie never gave up her faith in God. After the war, she dedicated her life to preaching about God's love and forgiveness, even toward those who had persecuted her. Her story is a testimony of what it means to surrender self-will for the sake of the Gospel.

Finally, Pastor David Wilkerson is another contemporary example of someone who gave up his own plans to follow God's will. Wilkerson left a comfortable rural church to go to the streets of New York, where he began ministering to gang members and drug addicts. Although he faced many challenges and dangers, his obedience led to the founding of "Teen Challenge," a ministry that has helped thousands of young people find freedom in Christ. His life and ministry are a powerful reminder that when we are willing to sacrifice our will, God can do extraordinary things through us.

Conclusion

The sacrifice of self-will is one of the most challenging but essential aspects of Christian discipleship. Throughout the Bible and church history, we find countless examples of people who were willing to give up their own plans and desires to follow God's will. Although this process often involves an internal struggle and significant sacrifices, obedience to God's will is the path to a full and meaningful life in Christ.

Following Christ means surrendering every aspect of our lives, including our desires, goals, and will. Through the sacrifice of self-will, we discover true freedom in Christ and experience the peace that only God can give. Though the cost is high, the eternal rewards far outweigh any temporary sacrifice we make. As followers of Christ, we are called to trust that God's plans are better than ours and to follow His will with faith, love, and obedience, knowing that in the end, His purpose will be fulfilled in our lives.

Chapter 6

The Spiritual Warfare of the Disciple

Introduction

The Christian life is not only a walk of faith and obedience but also a constant battle in the spiritual realm. In **Ephesians 6:12**, the apostle Paul writes, *"For our struggle is not against flesh and blood, but against the rulers, against the authorities, against the powers of this dark world and against the spiritual forces of evil in the heavenly realms."* As disciples of Christ, we are in the midst of a spiritual war that transcends what is visible and physical. This battle is ongoing and takes place in our hearts, our minds, and our surroundings, as the enemy tries to lead us away from God's purpose.

The spiritual warfare of the disciple should not be taken lightly. Although we have been redeemed by Christ and have the ultimate victory in Him, Satan still tries to discourage, distract, and destroy believers. The good news is that God has provided us with the tools and weapons we need to fight and win this battle. In this chapter, we will explore three key aspects of spiritual warfare: first, the spiritual battles faced by those who radically follow Christ; second, the biblical principles of spiritual warfare and resisting the enemy; and third, how we can equip ourselves for battle with the armor of God.

The Spiritual Battles Faced by Christ's Disciples

Radically following Christ automatically places us on the frontlines of spiritual warfare. The enemy is not interested in those who live comfortable and superficial lives, but in those who have decided to live for God in a committed and active way. In **1 Peter 5:8**, we are warned that *"your adversary the devil prowls around like a roaring lion, seeking someone to devour."* As committed disciples, we are targets of the enemy's attacks, who seeks to steal our peace, distort our faith, and lead us away from the truth of the Gospel.

One of the most common battles we face in spiritual warfare is the struggle against discouragement. The enemy knows that if he can discourage us, he can make us ineffective in our service to God. He often uses difficult circumstances, broken relationships, or personal failures to make us feel unworthy or incapable of fulfilling God's call. However, in **2 Corinthians 4:8-9**, Paul reminds us that although we are *"hard pressed on every side, but not crushed; perplexed, but not in despair; persecuted, but not abandoned; struck down, but not destroyed."* This promise strengthens us in the midst of the battle, knowing that God is with us and that we are not alone in our struggles.

Another area of spiritual battle is temptation. The enemy uses our weaknesses and sinful desires to try to lead us away from God. Even Jesus was tempted by Satan in the wilderness (**Matthew 4:1-11**), showing us that no one is exempt from temptation. However, Jesus showed us how to overcome it through the Word of God, responding to each temptation with Scripture. As disciples, we must be prepared to face temptation with the same weapons Jesus used: the truth of God's Word and reliance on the Holy Spirit.

Doubt is another powerful weapon that the enemy uses in spiritual warfare. In **Genesis 3**, we see how Satan sowed doubt in Eve's mind, questioning God's goodness and instructions. Doubt is one of the most effective ways the enemy diverts us from the path of faith. However, James 1:6 urges us to ask with faith, "without doubting," knowing that God is faithful to fulfill His promises. When we face doubt, we must anchor ourselves in God's Word, remembering that His truth is unchanging and that He will never fail us.

The battle for purity is another spiritual war faced by Christ's disciples. In a world saturated with sexual immorality and constant temptations, maintaining purity is a daily struggle. **1 Thessalonians 4:3-4** exhorts us, *"It is God's will that you should be sanctified: that you should avoid sexual immorality; that each of you should learn to control your own body in a way that is holy and honorable."* As disciples, we must be alert and disciplined in our decisions and behaviors, knowing that purity not only affects our relationship with God but also our testimony to others.

Finally, one of the most intense battles is the fight against distraction. The enemy uses all kinds of distractions to divert us from our mission in Christ. From materialism to technology, distraction is a subtle but effective tool to distract us from our purpose. In **Hebrews 12:1-2**, we are exhorted to *"throw off everything that hinders and the sin that so easily entangles, and let us run with perseverance the race marked out for us, fixing our eyes on Jesus."* Keeping our focus on

Christ is essential to overcoming this spiritual war and living lives that glorify God.

Biblical Principles of Spiritual Warfare and Resisting the Enemy

The Bible provides clear principles for facing and winning in spiritual warfare. One of the most fundamental principles is understanding that our battle is not against people, but against spiritual forces. In **Ephesians 6:12**, Paul reminds us that *"our struggle is not against flesh and blood,"* which is crucial for maintaining the perspective that our real battle is against Satan and his hosts. The enemy will try to make us believe that our struggles are with people, but we must remember that behind every spiritual conflict, there is a larger, unseen battle.

Another important principle is that spiritual warfare is fought with spiritual weapons, not with carnal ones. In **2 Corinthians 10:4**, we are told that *"the weapons we fight with are not the weapons of the world. On the contrary, they have divine power to demolish strongholds."* We cannot fight in our own strength or with human methods; we need the help of the Holy Spirit and the weapons God has provided. Prayer, the Word of God, and faith are our main tools in this battle, and we must use them diligently to resist the enemy's attacks.

Resisting the enemy is another key principle in spiritual warfare. In **James 4:7**, we are told, *"Submit yourselves, then, to God. Resist the devil, and he will flee from you."* Resistance is not passive; it requires an active stance of rejecting sin and the enemy's lies. Submitting to God is the key to resisting the devil. When we are under God's authority and live in obedience to His Word, the enemy has no power over us. This resistance is demonstrated through constant prayer, fasting, and the study of Scripture, tools that strengthen our faith and keep us alert in battle.

Prayer is one of the most powerful weapons in spiritual warfare. In **Ephesians 6:18**, Paul exhorts us to ***"pray in the Spirit on all occasions with all kinds of prayers and requests."*** Prayer connects us with God's power and equips us to face the enemy's attacks. Jesus Himself demonstrated the importance of prayer in His ministry, regularly praying before facing challenges and trials. When we pray, we activate God's protection and power over our lives, allowing us to resist spiritual attacks and remain firm in our faith.

Another essential principle is the importance of walking in holiness. Sin is an open door to the enemy's attacks. When we allow sin to remain in our lives, we give the devil an advantage in the battle. In **1 John 1:9**, we are promised that ***"if we confess our sins, he is faithful and just, he will forgive us our sins and purify us from all unrighteousness."*** Holiness is not just a matter of obedience but also protection. The closer we walk with God, the less ground we give the enemy to operate in our lives.

Finally, worship is another powerful weapon in spiritual warfare. In **2 Chronicles 20**, we see how King Jehoshaphat faced a war against powerful enemies, but instead of relying on his armies, he ordered the singers to praise God in the midst of the battle. Through worship, God confused the enemies and gave them victory. Worship has the power to change the spiritual atmosphere and to bring God's presence into our circumstances. When we worship God, we are declaring His lordship over our lives and our battles, disarming the enemy and strengthening ourselves in the Spirit.

Equipping Ourselves for Battle with the Armor of God

God has not left us unprotected in spiritual warfare; He has given us the armor we need to face the enemy's attacks. In **Ephesians 6:13-17**, Paul describes the armor of God as a set of spiritual tools that protect us and enable us to fight courageously. This armor is not optional but essential for every believer who wants to stand firm in the midst of the battle.

The first component of the armor is the belt of truth. Truth is fundamental in spiritual warfare because the enemy is the "father of lies" (**John 8:44**). If we are not rooted in the truth of God's Word, we are vulnerable to Satan's lies and deceptions. The belt of truth ensures that we stand firm in sound doctrine and that our lives are aligned with God's principles. Without truth, we have no solid foundation on which to build our faith.

The second component is the breastplate of righteousness. God's righteousness, granted through Jesus Christ, protects us from the enemy's attacks of guilt and condemnation. **Romans 8:1** says, *"There is now no condemnation for those who are in Christ Jesus."* The enemy will try to accuse us and make us feel unworthy, but the breastplate of righteousness reminds us that we are forgiven and that our standing before God depends not on our works but on Christ's perfect work on the cross. By walking in righteousness, we do not give the enemy room to attack us in areas of unconfessed sin.

The third component is the shoes of the gospel of peace. These enable us to stand firm in the proclamation of the Gospel and in the peace that surpasses all understanding. **Philippians 4:7** promises that *"the peace of God, which transcends all understanding, will guard your hearts and your minds in Christ Jesus."* Peace is both an offensive and defensive weapon in spiritual warfare. It allows us to remain calm and focused on God, even when the enemy tries to destabilize us with attacks of anxiety, fear, or confusion.

The fourth component is the shield of faith. In **Ephesians 6:16**, we are told that *"with the shield of faith you can extinguish all the flaming arrows of the evil one."* Faith is our defense against the enemy's attacks, especially in times of doubt or uncertainty. When the enemy throws attacks in the form of lies or temptations, we can use the shield of faith to remember God's promises and remain steadfast in our trust in His faithfulness. Faith gives us the ability to see beyond our present circumstances and trust in God's sovereign plan.

The fifth component is the helmet of salvation. The helmet protects our minds, which is one of the most important battlefields in spiritual warfare. In **Romans 12:2**, we are told to renew our minds to be able to discern God's will. The enemy will always seek to attack our minds with thoughts of doubt, condemnation, or confusion. However, the helmet of salvation reminds us that we are children of God, redeemed and secure in Christ. When our minds are protected by the truth of our salvation, we are able to resist the enemy's thoughts and lies.

Finally, the last component is the sword of the Spirit, which is the Word of God. Unlike the other components of the armor, which are mainly defensive, the sword of the Spirit is an offensive weapon. Jesus used the Word of God to overcome Satan's temptations in the wilderness (**Matthew 4:1-11**), and we must do the same. Memorizing and meditating on Scripture gives us the ability to respond to the enemy's attacks with God's truth. The Word of God is living and powerful (**Hebrews 4:12**), and when we use it in prayer and declaration, we destroy the enemy's strongholds and affirm ourselves in Christ's victory.

Conclusion

Spiritual warfare is a reality that every disciple of Christ faces in their walk of faith. While we are in a constant battle against the forces of evil, God has provided us with everything we need to overcome. Through prayer, God's Word, holiness, and faith, we are empowered to resist the enemy and stand firm in the midst of trials. The armor of God protects and equips us to face the enemy's attacks, reminding us that we are not alone in this battle but have the power of the Holy Spirit on our side.

As disciples, we are called to fight the good fight of faith (**1 Timothy 6:12**), knowing that the victory has already been won in Christ. Though we face challenges and temptations, we can be confident that in Christ, we are more than conquerors. By daily living with the armor of God, we can stand firm against the enemy's schemes, trusting that God will lead us to final victory. The disciple who understands the nature of spiritual warfare and equips themselves properly will not only withstand the enemy's attacks but will also advance the Kingdom of God in this world.

Chapter 7

The Reward of the Call

Introduction

Although following Christ involves sacrifice, renunciation, and a constant battle in the spiritual realm, there is also a promise of eternal rewards for those who persevere until the end. Jesus himself taught that there is a great reward for those who choose to deny themselves, take up their cross, and follow Him, even though this may involve suffering and opposition in this life. In **Matthew 19:29**, Jesus declared, *"And everyone who has left houses or brothers or sisters or father or mother or wife or children or fields for my sake will receive a hundred times as much and will inherit eternal life."* This verse is a powerful affirmation that the temporary sacrifice we make by following Christ will be abundantly rewarded, both in this life and in eternity.

However, it's important to remember that God's rewards don't always manifest in the way the world expects. The true reward of the call is not necessarily in earthly success or material blessings but in the spiritual and eternal blessings God has prepared for us. In this chapter, we will explore three key aspects of the reward of the call: first, the spiritual blessings we receive by following Christ; second, the joy and peace that come as a result of obedience; and third, the hope of eternal life that awaits us in the Kingdom of God.

The Spiritual Blessings We Receive by Following Christ

When we decide to follow Christ and respond to His call, we experience a deep transformation in our lives. One of the first rewards we receive is the gift of the Holy Spirit. In **Acts 2:38**, Peter said, *"Repent and be baptized, every one of you, in the name of Jesus Christ for the forgiveness of your sins. And you will receive the gift of the Holy Spirit."* The Holy Spirit is God's gift to all believers, and His presence in our lives fills us with power, wisdom, and guidance. Through the Holy Spirit, we experience a close and personal relationship with God, who guides us in every area of our lives.

Another spiritual blessing we receive by following Christ is adoption as children of God. In **Romans 8:15-16**, Paul writes, *"The Spirit you received does not make you slaves so that you live in fear again; rather, the Spirit you received brought about your adoption to sonship. And by him we cry, 'Abba, Father.' The Spirit himself testifies with our spirit that we are God's children."* Being children of God means we are no longer slaves to sin or to the fears of this world, but we are loved, accepted, and protected by our Heavenly Father. This identity as His children gives us deep security and confidence, knowing that we are part of God's family.

Another spiritual blessing is victory over sin and death. In **1 Corinthians 15:57**, Paul exclaims, *"But thanks be to God! He gives us the victory through our Lord Jesus*

Christ." Through Christ's work on the cross, we are no longer condemned to live under the power of sin or to fear death. Jesus paid the price for our sins and has given us victory over death, promising us eternal life. This victory gives us the freedom to live a full life, free from the chains of the past, and enables us to walk in the new identity we have received in Christ.

In addition to victory over sin, another spiritual reward we experience is growth in holiness. In **Philippians 1:6**, we are assured that ***"he who began a good work in you will carry it on to completion until the day of Christ Jesus."*** God is committed to our spiritual growth, and through His Spirit, He transforms us more and more into the image of His Son. This process of sanctification is a blessing in itself, as it allows us to live a life that reflects the character of Christ. As we grow in holiness, we experience greater freedom from sin and a deeper fullness in our relationship with God.

Another important aspect of spiritual blessings is the Christian community. By following Christ, we become part of the body of Christ, the church. In **Acts 2:42**, we are told that the first Christians "devoted themselves to the apostles' teaching and to fellowship, to the breaking of bread and to prayer. The Christian community is a blessing because it provides us with support, encouragement, and growth in our faith. We are not called to walk alone but to live in fellowship with other believers, sharing our burdens and encouraging one another in the Lord.

Finally, one of the greatest spiritual rewards we receive by following Christ is peace with God. **Romans 5:1** tells us, ***"Therefore, since we have been justified through*** *faith, we have peace with God through our Lord Jesus Christ."* This peace is not simply the absence of conflict but complete reconciliation with God. We are no longer separated from Him by our sins, but we have been reconciled through Christ. This inner peace is a fruit of our restored relationship with God, and it gives us a sense of security and well-being, even in the midst of trials and difficulties.

Joy and Peace as the Fruit of Obedience

Joy is another reward we receive by following Christ and obeying His call. Jesus said in **John 15:11**, *"I have told you this so that my joy may be in you and that your joy may be complete."* The joy that Jesus speaks of is not a temporary or superficial feeling but a deep and lasting joy that comes from living in communion with God and in obedience to His Word. This joy does not depend on our external circumstances but on our relationship with Christ. As we follow Jesus and live in obedience, we experience a joy that transcends the pain, suffering, and difficulties of life.

The believer's joy is also tied to the mission of sharing the Gospel with others. In **Luke 10:17**, we are told that the seventy disciples returned with joy after being sent out by Jesus to preach and heal. When we participate in God's work and see His Kingdom expand, we experience indescribable joy. The apostle Paul also experienced this joy when he saw the spiritual growth of the churches he had founded. In **1 Thessalonians 2:19-20**, he writes, *"For what is our hope, our joy, or the crown in which we will glory in the presence of our Lord Jesus when he comes? Is it not you? Indeed, you are our glory and joy."* By obeying God's call and participating in the work of His Kingdom, we experience a joy that surpasses any earthly satisfaction.

Peace is another fruit of obedience to God. In **Isaiah 26:3**, we are told, *"You will keep in perfect peace those whose minds are steadfast, because they trust in you."* The peace that God gives does not depend on our circumstances but on our trust in Him. As we learn to trust God and obey His will, we experience peace that surpasses all understanding (**Philippians 4:7**). This peace is one of the greatest rewards of following Christ, as it enables us to face life's difficulties with serenity and confidence, knowing that God is in control.

Another aspect of joy and peace is the rest we find in Christ. In **Matthew 11:28-29**, Jesus said, *"Come to me, all you who are weary and burdened, and I will give you rest. Take my yoke upon you and learn from me, for I am gentle and humble in heart, and you will find rest for your souls."* When we obey Christ's call and surrender our burdens to Him, we find rest and relief from our worries. This rest is not just physical but a deep rest for the soul, where we can trust that God cares for us and that our lives are in His hands.

Joy and peace also manifest in our relationships with others. In **Galatians 5:22-23**, the fruit of the Spirit is described, including joy and peace, as well as love, patience, and kindness. As we grow in our obedience to God and in our relationship with the Holy Spirit, these fruits manifest in our lives, not only for our own benefit but to bless others. Obedience to God produces a transformed character, reflecting the love and peace of Christ in our relationships, in our families, and in our communities.

Finally, joy and peace are signs that we are walking in God's will. In **Psalm 16:11**, the psalmist declares, *"You make known to me the path of life; you will fill me with joy in your presence, with eternal pleasures at your right hand."* When we obey God, we walk in His presence, and in His presence, we find the fullness of joy and peace. This joy and peace are not temporary but eternal, for they come from a continuous and deep relationship with the Creator. As we walk in obedience, we experience closer communion with God, filling us with joy and peace in every season of life.

The Hope of Eternal Life in God's Kingdom

One of the most glorious rewards of Christ's call is the hope of eternal life. In **John 14:2-3**, Jesus promised, *"My Father's house has many rooms; if that were not so, would I have told you that I am going there to prepare a place for you? And if I go and prepare a place for you, I will come back and take you to be with me that you also may be where I am."* Eternal life is the culmination of our hope as Christians and is the final reward for those who persevere in faith and follow Christ until the end. This hope gives us an eternal perspective that transforms how we live here on earth.

Eternal life is not just a future concept but a present reality for believers. In **John 17:3**, Jesus defines eternal life as *"that they know you, the only true God, and Jesus Christ, whom you have sent."* Eternal life begins the moment we enter a relationship with God through Jesus Christ. It's not just about life after death but about living in communion with God here and now. This intimate relationship with the Father is the essence of eternal life, and it is the greatest reward we can receive by following Christ.

In addition to the hope of eternal life, believers also have the promise of a heavenly inheritance. In **1 Peter 1:4**, we are told of *"an inheritance that can never perish, spoil or fade. This inheritance is kept in heaven for you."* This inheritance cannot be destroyed or corrupted by the sin or decay of the world. It is an eternal reward that God has prepared for those who love and obey Him. This inheritance includes the fullness of life in God's presence, perfect communion with the saints, and participation in the eternal Kingdom of Christ.

The hope of eternal life also strengthens us in the midst of life's trials and tribulations. In **2 Corinthians 4:17-18**, Paul writes, *"For our light and momentary troubles are achieving for us an eternal glory that far outweighs them all. So we fix our eyes not on what is seen, but on what is unseen, since what is seen is temporary, but what is unseen is eternal."* By keeping our eyes fixed on eternal things, we can endure hardships and suffering, knowing that our trials are temporary, and that eternal glory awaits us in the presence of God.

Another glorious promise related to eternal life is the resurrection of the dead. In **1 Corinthians 15:52**, we are told that *"in a flash, in the twinkling of an eye, at the last trumpet... the dead will be raised imperishable, and we will be changed."* The resurrection is the culmination of our salvation, where our mortal bodies will be transformed into glorified bodies, free from sin and disease. This hope gives us comfort and encouragement, especially when we face the loss of loved ones. We know that death does not have the final word because, in Christ, we have the promise of resurrection and eternal life.

Finally, the hope of eternal life also includes the reward of reigning with Christ in His eternal Kingdom. In **Revelation 3:21**, Jesus promises, *"To the one who is victorious, I will give the right to sit with me on my throne, just as I was victorious and sat down with my Father on his throne."* As followers of Christ, we are not only called to be saved but to reign with Him in His Kingdom. This is an incredible reward that God has prepared for His children, and it is a reminder that our faithfulness to Christ in this life has eternal implications in the coming Kingdom.

Conclusion

The reward of the call is a profound and glorious reality for those who have chosen to follow Christ. While the path of discipleship may be difficult and filled with challenges, the spiritual rewards, the joy and peace we experience in this life, and the hope of eternal life far outweigh any temporary sacrifice. God, in His grace, has prepared great blessings for His children, both in this life and in eternity, and He invites us to walk in obedience to experience His fullness.

Following Christ not only transforms our present life but also assures us of a glorious future in God's presence. As disciples, we are called to keep our eyes fixed on the eternal rewards, knowing that our faithfulness to Christ will be rewarded beyond what we can imagine. In Christ, we have the promise of abundant life, peace that surpasses all understanding, and the certainty that our hope is secure in God's eternal Kingdom.

Chapter 8

The Call to Serve: The Example of Christ

Introduction

One of the most transformative aspects of the Christian call is the call to serve. Jesus, the Son of God, came to earth not to be served but to serve and to give His life as a ransom for many (**Mark 10:45**). His example of selfless and sacrificial service is the model for all who follow Him. Throughout His ministry, Jesus demonstrated that true greatness is not found in power or prestige but in the willingness to humble oneself and serve others. In **John 13:14-15**, after washing His disciples' feet, Jesus said to them, *"Now that I, your Lord and Teacher, have washed your feet, you also should wash one another's feet. I have set you an example that you should do as I have done for you."*

The call to serve is not optional for the disciple of Christ, but an essential part of following Jesus. Through service, we reflect the character of Christ and extend His love and compassion to others. In this chapter, we will explore three aspects of the call to serve: first, Jesus as the ultimate example of service; second, the importance of a servant's heart in discipleship; and third, examples of biblical leaders who served without seeking recognition.

The Cost of the Call

Diego Colón Batiz

Jesus as the Ultimate Example of Service

Jesus is the supreme example of what it means to serve others. Throughout the Gospels, we see how Jesus ministered to the crowds, healing the sick, delivering the oppressed, and teaching the lost. Although Jesus had all power and authority as the Son of God, He chose to humble Himself and serve humanity in ways that defied the cultural and religious expectations of His time. **Philippians 2:6-7** tell us that *"He made Himself nothing, taking the very nature of a servant, being made in human likeness."* Jesus did not come to earth seeking exaltation for Himself, but to fulfill the Father's will and serve others.

One of the most powerful moments in Jesus' life that demonstrates His willingness to serve was when He washed His disciples' feet. In **John 13**, Jesus knelt before them and performed a task usually reserved for servants. This act of humility and service surprised the disciples, especially Peter, who initially refused to let Jesus wash his feet. However, Jesus explained that this act was an example of how they should treat one another. This moment was not only an act of service but also a profound teaching about the nature of leadership in God's Kingdom: the greatest among us is the one willing to serve others.

Another example of Jesus' service was His compassion for the crowds. **Matthew 14:14**, says, *"When Jesus landed and saw a large crowd, He had compassion on them and healed their sick."* Although Jesus was tired and seeking a place to rest, His love for people led Him to meet their physical and spiritual needs. Jesus' service was not motivated by obligation, but by a deep love and compassion for others. This is a key lesson for us as disciples: true service flows from a heart full of love for God and others.

In addition to His public ministry, Jesus also served in private. He often withdrew to solitary places, not only to recharge but also to intercede for those He ministered to. In **Luke 22:32**, Jesus said to Peter, *"But I have prayed for you, Simon, that your faith may not fail."* This is a reminder that service is not always visible or recognized by others, but it is equally important. Jesus teaches us that serving others includes interceding for them in prayer and being willing to sacrifice our time and energy in secret for their well-being.

Another aspect of Jesus' service was His willingness to minister to those society rejected. In **Mark 2:16-17**, Jesus was criticized for eating with tax collectors and sinners, but He responded by saying, *"It is not the healthy who need a doctor, but the sick. I have not come to call the righteous, but sinners."* Jesus did not discriminate between people; He served both the rich and the poor, the righteous and the sinners. His service broke down social and religious barriers, demonstrating that God's love and grace are available to all, regardless of their status or past.

Finally, Jesus' ultimate act of service was His sacrifice on the cross. In **John 15:13**, Jesus said, *"Greater love has no one than this: to lay down one's life for one's friends."* Jesus did not just serve others during His earthly ministry; He gave His life for all humanity. His death on the cross was the greatest act of service ever performed, as through His sacrifice, He offered redemption and eternal life to all who believe in Him. As followers of Christ, we are called to imitate

His example of service, knowing that the greatest service we can offer is to sacrifice our lives, time, and resources for the well-being of others.

The Importance of a Servant's Heart in Discipleship

Christian discipleship is not only about learning doctrine or attending church; it is about developing a servant's heart, willing to put the needs of others above our own. In **Matthew 20:26-28**, Jesus said to His disciples, *"Whoever wants to become great among you must be your servant, and whoever wants to be first must be your slave—just as the Son of Man did not come to be served, but to serve."* This teaching challenges cultural notions of greatness and power, and calls us to follow Jesus' example, serving with humility and love.

A servant's heart is not born out of obligation or duty, but from an internal transformation that occurs when the Holy Spirit works in our lives. In **2 Corinthians 5:14**, Paul declares, *"For Christ's love compels us."* True service flows from Christ's love in us. When we understand how much Jesus has loved and served us, we are compelled to serve others with that same love. Service is not a burden when it is motivated by love, but a natural expression of our gratitude to God and our compassion for others.

The willingness to serve is also a mark of spiritual maturity. In **Philippians 2:3-4**, we are exhorted, *"Do nothing out of selfish ambition or vain conceit. Rather, in humility value others above yourselves, not looking to your own interests but each of you to the interests of the others."* A servant's heart seeks the welfare of others, not out of pride or to gain recognition, but because it values others as more important than itself. This type of service reflects the character of Christ and shows the fruit of a disciple who has been transformed by God's grace.

Humility is another essential component of a servant's heart. Jesus taught us that to be great in God's Kingdom, we must humble ourselves and serve as He did. In **Mark 9:35**, Jesus said, *"Anyone who wants to be first must be the very last, and the servant of all."* Humility leads us to recognize that we are not superior to anyone and that every person, regardless of their status or position, deserves our respect and service. A disciple with a servant's heart does not seek to exalt themselves, but delights in exalting others and serving them with love.

A servant's heart is also manifested in the willingness to serve in any place or circumstance, without expecting recognition or rewards. In **Colossians 3:23-24**, we are told, *"Whatever you do, work at it with all your heart, as working for the Lord, not for human masters, since you know that you will receive an inheritance from the Lord as a reward. It is the Lord Christ you are serving."* A true servant of Christ does not seek the applause or approval of men, but serves with the motivation of pleasing God. This type of service is authentic and consistent, because it is not dependent on external circumstances but on an intimate relationship with God.

Finally, service is a powerful tool for growth in discipleship. When we serve others, God works in our hearts, molding us into the image of Christ. **James 1:22** tells us that we must be *"doers of the word, and not hearers only."* Service is a way to put into practice what we have learned from the Scriptures. Through service, God reveals areas in our lives that need transformation, and gives us opportunities to grow in faith, patience, and compassion. A disciple committed to service experiences constant and profound transformation in their relationship with God and with others.

Examples of Biblical Leaders Who Served Without Seeking Recognition

Throughout Scripture, we see examples of leaders who served God and His people with humility, without seeking recognition or personal glory. One such leader was Moses. Although Moses was called to lead Israel out of slavery in Egypt and through the wilderness, he never sought power or fame for himself. **Numbers 12:3** tells us that *"Moses was a very humble man, more than anyone else on the face of the earth."* His humility and willingness to serve God and the people of Israel, even in the midst of great difficulties, made him a powerful leader. Moses always directed the glory to God and served with deep dependence on Him.

Another example is Joseph, who served faithfully and humbly, even when he was betrayed and unjustly imprisoned. Instead of becoming bitter or seeking revenge, Joseph continued to serve where God had placed him, trusting that the Lord was working in every situation. **Genesis 39:21** tells us that *"the Lord was with Joseph; he showed him kindness and granted him favor in the eyes of the prison warden."* Joseph's willingness to serve, even in adversity, led him to be elevated to a position of great responsibility in Egypt, where he was ultimately used by God to save many lives.

The prophet Samuel is another example of a leader who served without seeking personal recognition. From his youth, Samuel was dedicated to the service of the Lord, and throughout his life, he served as a judge, prophet, and leader in Israel. In 1 **Samuel 3:10**, we see his willingness to serve when he responded to God's call, saying, *"Speak, for your servant is listening."* Samuel served God and the people of Israel with integrity and faithfulness, never seeking to exalt himself. His life was an example of obedience and selfless service to God.

Another biblical leader who served with humility was Nehemiah. Though he was the cupbearer to the king in Persia, a position of great influence, Nehemiah did not let his position prevent him from serving his people. When he learned that the walls of Jerusalem were in ruins, Nehemiah left his comfortable position at the royal court and devoted himself to rebuilding the city. In **Nehemiah 2:17**, he said to the people, *"You see the trouble we are in: Jerusalem lies in ruins, and its gates have been burned with fire. Come, let us rebuild the wall of Jerusalem, and we will no longer be in disgrace."* Nehemiah worked side by side with the people, showing that a true leader is willing to get their hands dirty for the good of others.

In the New Testament, the apostle Paul is an example of someone who served without seeking recognition. Although he was an apostle and the founder of many churches, Paul always considered himself a servant of Christ and of others. In **1 Corinthians 9:19**, he wrote, *"Though I am free and belong to no one, I have made myself a slave to everyone, to win as many as possible."* Paul dedicated his life to serving the Gospel, facing persecution, imprisonment, and hardship, but he never sought glory for himself. His desire was that Christ be exalted and that others come to know the salvation in Jesus.

Finally, Timothy is another example of a leader who served with humility. Although he was young and faced many challenges in ministry, Timothy was always willing to serve wherever needed. In **Philippians 2:20-21**, Paul wrote, *"I have no one else like him, who will show genuine concern for your welfare. For everyone looks out for their own interests, not those of Jesus Christ."* Timothy distinguished himself by his willingness to put the needs of others above his own, showing the heart of a true servant of Christ.

The call to serve is one of the most essential aspects of Christian discipleship. Jesus, our Savior and ultimate example, showed us that true greatness is found in the willingness to humble oneself and serve others. Through service, we reflect the character of Christ and extend His love to a world in need. Service is not just an external action but an internal attitude that flows from a heart transformed by the love of God.

As disciples of Christ, we are called to follow His example, developing a servant's heart that delights in putting the needs of others above our own. We do not serve for recognition or approval, but to glorify God and build up His people. Through service, we not only bless others but also experience deep spiritual growth and closer communion with our Lord. A life of service is a fulfilling life, for in serving others, we find our true purpose and reflect the love of Christ to the world.

Chapter 9

Persecution and Rejection: The Path of the Disciple

Introduction

Persecution and rejection have been a constant reality for followers of Christ since the beginning of Christianity. Jesus left no doubt about this aspect when He said, *"Remember what I told you: 'A servant is not greater than his master.' If they persecuted me, they will persecute you also"* (**John 15:20**). Being a disciple of Christ means living in opposition to the world's system, and this opposition often manifests in persecution, rejection, and misunderstanding. This suffering is part of the cost of following Jesus, but it is a cost we are called to bear with courage and trust in God's promises.

While persecution can take many forms, from mockery and social rejection to imprisonment and martyrdom, Christ's disciples find comfort in the promises of God. Jesus assured us that though we would face trouble in this world, He has overcome the world (**John 16:33**). In this chapter, we will explore three aspects of the disciple's journey through persecution and rejection: first, how to face persecution and rejection for the sake of the Gospel; second, the promises of Jesus for those who are persecuted; and third, examples from the early church of their perseverance in the face of rejection.

How to Face Persecution and Rejection for the Sake of the Gospel

Facing persecution and rejection is not easy, but it is an integral part of Christian discipleship. Jesus warned us that following Him would mean going against the flow of the world. In **Matthew 5:10-12**, Jesus pronounced a blessing on those who are persecuted for righteousness' sake, saying, *"Blessed are those who are persecuted because of righteousness, for theirs is the kingdom of heaven. Blessed are you when people insult you, persecute you and falsely say all kinds of evil against you because of me. Rejoice and be glad, because great is your reward in heaven."* Though persecution brings pain and suffering, Jesus calls us to rejoice in it, for our reward in heaven is great.

The first key to facing persecution is to understand that we are not the first or the only ones to experience it. Throughout history, followers of Christ have been persecuted, from the apostles to the martyrs of the early church and even Christians today facing persecution in many parts of the world. In **2 Timothy 3:12**, Paul says, *"In fact, everyone who wants to live a godly life in Christ Jesus will be persecuted."* Persecution is a distinguishing mark of true disciples of Christ. Remembering that we are part of a long line of believers who have endured suffering for their faith helps us find the strength to persevere.

Another way to face persecution is by remembering that when the world rejects us, we are being identified with Christ. In **John 15:18**, Jesus said, *"If the world hates you, keep in mind that it hated me first."* Being rejected for the sake of the Gospel is an honor because it unites us with Christ in His suffering. Peter encourages us not to be surprised when we face trials, but to *"rejoice inasmuch as you participate in the sufferings of Christ"* (**1 Peter 4:13**). Though the world may reject us, we have the assurance that God accepts us and will reward us for our faithfulness.

Prayer is another powerful tool for facing persecution. In **Acts 4:29**, the early Christians prayed, *"Now, Lord, consider their threats and enable your servants to speak your word with great boldness."* Rather than asking for persecution to cease, they prayed for boldness to continue preaching the Gospel. When we face persecution, we should turn to God in prayer, asking for strength, courage, and perseverance to remain faithful to our calling. Prayer not only strengthens us but also reminds us that God is with us in the midst of trials and that His grace is sufficient to sustain us.

Additionally, we must learn to love and pray for those who persecute us. Jesus taught us to *"love your enemies and pray for those who persecute you"* (**Matthew 5:44**). This command is difficult, but it is essential to reflecting the character of Christ. By loving our enemies and praying for them, we not only overcome evil with good (**Romans 12:21**), but we also open the door for God to work in their hearts and bring them to salvation.

Finally, we must keep our hope in the promises of God. In **1 Peter 5:10**, we are assured that *"after you have suffered a little while, He Himself will restore you and make you strong, firm and steadfast."* Persecution is temporary, but God's promises are eternal. When we keep our eyes on the eternal rewards that await us, we can endure trials with patience and perseverance. We know that, though the world rejects us, God is preparing a crown of glory for those who remain faithful to the end.

The Promises of Jesus for Those Who Are Persecuted

Jesus not only warned us about the persecution we would face, but He also gave us precious promises for those who suffer for His sake. One of the most significant promises is that we will be rewarded in heaven. In **Matthew 5:12**, Jesus said, *"Rejoice and be glad, because great is your reward in heaven."* Though persecution brings temporary suffering, Jesus assures us that an eternal reward awaits us in heaven. This promise gives us the strength to endure trials, knowing that our hardships are not in vain.

Another promise is that Jesus is with us in the midst of persecution. In **Matthew 28:20**, Jesus promised, *"And surely I am with you always, to the very end of the age."* This promise gives us deep assurance, knowing that we do not face persecution alone. Jesus, who experienced rejection and persecution in its most intense form, is with us in every moment of our struggle. His presence strengthens and comforts us, reminding us that He is our refuge and our defender.

Jesus also promised that, though we may be rejected by the world, we will be accepted and honored by the Father. In **Matthew 10:32-33**, Jesus said, *"Whoever acknowledges me before others, I will also acknowledge before my Father in heaven. But whoever disowns me before others, I will disown before my Father in heaven."* This promise assures us that when we are faithful to Christ, He intercedes for us before the Father, and we are honored in God's presence, even if the world despises us.

One of the most comforting promises is that persecution is a means by which God strengthens and purifies us. In **James 1:2-4**, we are exhorted to *"consider it pure joy, my brothers and sisters, whenever you face trials of many kinds, because you know that the testing of your faith produces perseverance."* God uses persecution to perfect our character and increase our dependence on Him. Though persecution may be painful, it is an opportunity for us to grow in faith, perseverance, and spiritual maturity. Every trial we face draws us closer to the image of Christ and prepares us for the glory that is to come.

Jesus also promised that, despite persecution, His Kingdom would prevail. In **Matthew 16:18**, He said, *"I will build my church, and the gates of Hades will not overcome it."* Though followers of Christ face opposition and persecution in this world, the Kingdom of God advances with power. The church has endured centuries of persecution, yet it continues to grow and expand throughout the world. This promise gives us confidence that, though we face difficulties, we are on the victorious side, and God's Kingdom will be fully established when Christ returns.

Finally, Jesus promised that those who remain faithful until the end will receive the crown of life. In **Revelation 2:10**, we are told, *"Be faithful, even to the point of death, and I will give you life as your victor's crown."* This promise encourages us to persevere in the face of persecution, knowing that there is an eternal reward for those who remain faithful. Though the world may take away our comfort, our status, or even our lives, it cannot take away the eternal life that Jesus has secured for us. This hope gives us the strength to press on, trusting in the promises of our Savior.

Examples of the Early Church's Perseverance in the Face of Rejection

The early church is a powerful testimony of how followers of Christ can persevere through persecution and rejection with courage and faith. From its beginnings, the church faced intense opposition from both religious authorities and the Roman Empire. Yet despite the persecution, the early Christians remained faithful to their calling and continued to preach the Gospel with boldness. In **Acts 5:41**, we are told that the apostles, after being flogged and threatened, ***"left the Sanhedrin, rejoicing because they had been counted worthy of suffering disgrace for the Name."*** Their joy in the midst of suffering is an example of the strength and courage God grants to His faithful servants.

One of the most inspiring examples of the early church's perseverance is Stephen, the first Christian martyr. In **Acts 7**, Stephen was brought before the Sanhedrin, and despite the accusations against him, he boldly preached the truth of the Gospel. As he was being stoned, Stephen prayed, ***"Lord, do not hold this sin against them"*** (**Acts 7:60**), showing a heart full of grace and love, even toward his enemies. His death was not in vain, as his testimony left a deep impact on Saul of Tarsus, who would later become the apostle Paul.

Another notable example is the apostle Peter, who was imprisoned multiple times for preaching the Gospel. In **Acts 12**, we learn that Peter was arrested and placed under heavy guard, but *"the church was earnestly praying to God for him"* (**Acts 12:5**). Through prayer, God intervened and miraculously freed Peter from prison. This episode reminds us that while persecution is real, God's power is even greater, and He can intervene in surprising ways to protect and deliver His servants.

Paul is another example of a leader of the early church who faced tremendous persecution yet remained faithful to his calling. In **2 Corinthians 11:23-28**, Paul describes some of the trials he faced, including imprisonments, beatings, shipwrecks, and constant dangers. Yet despite all he suffered, Paul never stopped preaching the Gospel or serving the churches. In **2 Timothy 4:7**, Paul said, *"I have fought the good fight, I have finished the race, I have kept the faith."* His life is a testimony of perseverance in the face of persecution and the joy that comes from serving Christ, even in the most difficult circumstances.

The apostle John is another notable example of the persecution suffered by the early disciples. Though he did not die as a martyr, John was exiled to the island of Patmos because of his preaching of the Gospel and his faithful testimony of Christ. In **Revelation 1:9**, John writes, *"I, John, your brother and companion in the suffering and kingdom and patient endurance that are ours in Jesus, was on the island of Patmos because of the word of God and the testimony of Jesus."* Despite being in a place of isolation and exile, John received one of the most powerful revelations in church history: the vision of the Book of Revelation. His example teaches us that even in the midst of persecution and isolation, God continues to work and reveal His purposes to those who remain faithful.

Finally, the martyrs of the early church, such as those mentioned earlier, inspire believers to remain faithful to the end. The willingness of the apostles and early Christians to suffer persecution and even death for the sake of Christ is a testimony that has endured through the centuries. These men and women saw rejection and persecution not as a defeat but as an opportunity to glorify God and testify to the power of the Gospel. Today, their lives remind us that the call to follow Christ often means facing opposition, but the eternal rewards far outweigh the temporary suffering.

In conclusion, the path of the disciple of Christ is marked by persecution and rejection, but it is also filled with the promises of God and the comfort of His presence. Throughout history, the followers of Jesus have faced the world's opposition but remained faithful to their calling, trusting that God is faithful to reward those who persevere. Though persecution brings pain, it also brings blessings and a deeper communion with Christ, who suffered for us and left us the example to follow.

As disciples, we are called to face persecution with courage, love, and prayer, trusting in God's promises and the reward that awaits us in heaven. Though the world may reject us, we know that we are accepted by God and that our tribulations are not in vain. Faithfulness in the midst of persecution not only glorifies God but also strengthens our faith and prepares us for eternal glory. Christ's call is clear: *"Be faithful, even to the point of death, and I will give you the crown of life"* **(Revelation 2:10).**

Chapter 10

Forsaking All: The Testimony of the Apostles

Introduction

The call to follow Christ is not a half-hearted commitment or a mere religious affiliation; it is a radical invitation to forsake everything for the love of Jesus. In **Luke 14:33**, Jesus said, *"So likewise, whoever of you does not forsake all that he has cannot be My disciple."* This challenging statement reveals that true discipleship requires a complete surrender where Christ becomes our highest priority above our possessions, relationships, and personal desires. The call to forsake all is not a suggestion but an unavoidable demand for those who wish to follow Christ.

The clearest example of what it means to forsake everything is found in the apostles, who left their homes, jobs, and families to follow Jesus. Their willingness to abandon everything for the Kingdom of God is a powerful testimony of what radical discipleship entails. In this chapter, we will explore three key aspects of the call to forsake all: first, how the apostles left everything to follow Jesus; second, reflections on what it means to forsake the material, emotional, and spiritual for the Kingdom of God; and third, modern examples of people who have done so.

The Cost of the Call

Diego Colón Batiz

How the Apostles Left Everything to Follow Jesus

The apostles of Jesus demonstrate what it means to forsake everything for the Kingdom of God. In **Luke 5:11**, we are told that Peter, Andrew, James, and John *"left everything and followed Him."* These men were fishermen with established families and livelihoods, but when Jesus called them, they did not hesitate to abandon their nets and boats to follow Him. The apostles' decision was radical, as it meant leaving behind not only their economic means but also the security and stability of their lives. This act of obedience shows that following Jesus requires total surrender and a willingness to trust Him fully for our needs.

The calling of Matthew, the tax collector, is another example of someone who forsook everything to follow Jesus. In **Matthew 9:9**, we are told that Jesus *"saw a man named Matthew sitting at the tax collector's booth. 'Follow me,' He told him, and Matthew got up and followed Him."* Matthew had a lucrative position as a tax collector, but he left it all to follow Christ. His willingness to give up a comfortable career and a life of wealth demonstrates that the call to follow Jesus involves being willing to sacrifice even the things the world considers most valuable.

Another inspiring example is that of Elisha, who left his life as a farmer to follow the prophet Elijah. In **1 Kings 19:19-21**, Elijah threw his cloak over Elisha, symbolizing God's call upon his life. Elisha responded by sacrificing the oxen he was using and burning the plowing equipment, thus showing his total renunciation of his old life to follow the prophetic call. His willingness to leave everything behind is a powerful example of how God's call may require us to forsake even our most cherished occupations and relationships to fulfill His purpose.

Abraham is another notable example in Scripture, who obeyed God's call to leave his country, his people, and his father's household without knowing exactly where he was going (**Genesis 12:1**). Abraham left a comfortable and stable life in Ur of the Chaldeans to follow God's promise to an unknown land. His faith and obedience earned him the title "father of faith," and his willingness to forsake everything to follow God is a key testimony for all believers. The sacrifice Abraham made by leaving everything is a reminder that God's call always requires faith and often involves leaving behind the known and comfortable.

Moses also serves as an example of someone who forsook a life of comfort to follow God's call. Though he had been raised in Pharaoh's palace, Moses chose to identify with the Israelites, the slaves of Egypt, and eventually led them to freedom. **Hebrews 11:24-26** says, *"By faith Moses, when he had grown up, refused to be known as the son of Pharaoh's daughter. He chose to be mistreated along with the people of God rather than to enjoy the fleeting pleasures of sin."* Moses forsook power, wealth, and privilege to fulfill the mission God had given him, a clear example of how God's call demands us to forsake everything for His cause.

Finally, the apostle Paul also exemplifies the cost of following Christ. Before his conversion, Paul was a Pharisee with prestigious education and high status within Judaism. However, after his encounter with Jesus on the road to Damascus, Paul considered everything he once valued as "rubbish" compared to the surpassing worth of knowing Christ (**Philippians 3:8**). From that moment on, Paul forsook his earthly status and ambitions to fully dedicate himself to the service of Christ, traveling, preaching, and suffering for the Gospel until the end of his life.

Reflections on What It Means to Forsake the Material, Emotional, and Spiritual for the Kingdom of God

Forsaking everything for Christ is not just about leaving behind our material possessions; it involves a total surrender of all areas of our lives. First, forsaking the material means that we are willing to sacrifice our possessions, our comfort, and our financial security for the love of Christ. In **Mark 10:21**, Jesus said to the rich young ruler, *"Go, sell everything you have and give to the poor, and you will have treasure in heaven. Then come, follow me."* Though the rich young ruler was unwilling to make that sacrifice, Jesus calls us to be willing to place Him above any material possession. This type of renunciation challenges us to trust God completely as our provider, knowing that He will supply all our needs according to His riches in glory (**Philippians 4:19**).

Forsaking the material also means learning to live with contentment regardless of our economic circumstances. In **Philippians 4:12-13**, Paul said, *"I know what it is to be in need, and I know what it is to have plenty. I have learned the secret of being content in any and every situation, whether well-fed or hungry, whether living in plenty or in want. I can do all this through Him who gives me strength."* This passage shows us that contentment does not depend on what we possess but on our trust in Christ. Forsaking the material means being willing to live with less if that is what God requires of us and finding our satisfaction in Him, not in the things of this world.

Second, forsaking the emotional means that we are willing to surrender our relationships and personal desires to God. In **Luke 14:26**, Jesus said, *"If anyone comes to Me and does not hate father and mother, wife and children, brothers and sisters—yes, even their own life—such a person cannot be My disciple."* Though this passage may seem harsh, Jesus is not calling us to hate our loved ones but to place Him above all our relationships. Following Christ may mean facing opposition from our families or friends or having to choose between our relationships and our loyalty to Christ. This emotional renunciation is difficult but essential for being true disciples of Jesus.

Forsaking the emotional also involves trusting that God has a perfect plan for our lives, even when our emotions pull us in another direction. Often, our desires and emotions lead us to seek our own satisfaction and happiness, but Jesus calls us to surrender those desires to Him and trust that His plan is better than ours. **Psalm 37:4** tells us, *"Take delight in the Lord, and He will give you the desires of your heart."* When we surrender our emotions and desires to God, we discover that His will is perfect and that He will bless us in ways beyond what we can imagine.

Finally, forsaking the spiritual means that we are willing to surrender our ambitions and dreams to God. Sometimes, even in the spiritual realm, we can have selfish desires or ambitions that are not aligned with God's plan for our lives. In **Galatians 2:20**, Paul declared, *"I have been* *crucified with Christ, and I no longer live, but Christ lives in me."* Forsaking the spiritual means being willing to die to ourselves and our ambitions, allowing Christ to live and work through us. This is an act of total surrender, where we trust that God's plans are better than ours, even in the spiritual realm.

Forsaking the spiritual also means embracing suffering and sacrifice for the Kingdom of God. In **Romans 12:1**, we are exhorted to present our bodies as *"a living sacrifice, holy and pleasing to God."* This call to be a living sacrifice implies a willingness to suffer for the sake of Christ and to sacrifice our comforts, desires, and plans for the sake of the Gospel. Though sacrifice is painful, it is also the pathway to true freedom in Christ, because when we die to ourselves, we experience the abundant life He has promised us.

Ultimately, forsaking everything for Christ is a call to total obedience. In **John 14:15**, Jesus said, *"If you love Me, keep My commands."* Obedience is the mark of a true disciple, and forsaking everything means that we are willing to obey Christ in every area of our lives, even when we do not understand His plan or when His will goes against our desires. This radical obedience is the fruit of a deep relationship with Christ, where we trust that He is our Lord and Savior and that His will is always for our good.

Modern Examples of People Who Have Done This

A modern example is Hudson Taylor, a British missionary who forsook his life in England to bring the Gospel to China in the 19th century. Taylor adopted Chinese customs and dress, something revolutionary at the time, to identify with the Chinese people and win their trust. Though he faced illness, the death of loved ones, and many financial difficulties, Hudson Taylor never ceased trusting in God's provision and his calling to serve in China. His life is a testimony of sacrifice and total surrender for the love of the Kingdom.

Taylor founded the China Inland Mission, which sent hundreds of missionaries to the most remote areas of that country, facing enormous risks. Throughout his life, he witnessed financial and spiritual miracles as he trusted completely in God to meet every need of his ministry. Although he lost several children and faced opposition both inside and outside the church, he never strayed from following God's call. For him, forsaking all that was earthly was the key to a ministry that continues to influence the evangelization of China today.

Another example is Lottie Moon, a Southern Baptist missionary who served in China for almost 40 years. Lottie left behind her home and family to live among the Chinese, serving them during times of famine and war. During a hunger crisis, she shared her own food with the needy until her health began to fail dramatically. Lottie died from malnutrition while serving the Chinese, but her legacy lives on through the "Lottie Moon Christmas Offering," which supports missions around the world. Her life reflects what it means to give everything, even one's own life, for the love of Christ and others.

In more recent times, Heidi Baker, a missionary in Mozambique, forsook a comfortable life to serve in one of the poorest countries in the world. Along with her husband, she founded Iris Global, a ministry that has planted thousands of churches and cares for orphans and marginalized people. Heidi has faced disease, civil wars, and persecution, but she has never abandoned her calling to follow Christ among the poorest. Her life is an example of what it means to forsake not only material comforts but also personal safety to bring the Gospel to difficult places.

Heidi has witnessed extraordinary miracles in her ministry, from healings to the multiplication of food to feed thousands. But what stands out in her life is her dedication to unconditional love. Heidi preaches and lives a radical gospel of love and compassion, demonstrating that following Christ also means caring for the physical and emotional needs of others. Her willingness to forsake everything and trust in God's provision and protection has led her to impact millions of lives in Mozambique and beyond.

Another contemporary example is Brother Yun, known as "The Heavenly Man," a Chinese Christian who has suffered intense persecution for his faith. Arrested and imprisoned multiple times, Yun was tortured but never renounced his faith. While imprisoned, he preached the Gospel and continued trusting in God. His story is a testimony of how, even when physical freedom is forsaken, God uses the willingness to suffer for His cause to bring His message to places others cannot reach.

Finally, Jackie Pullinger, a British missionary in Hong Kong, left her secure life in England to work among drug addicts and marginalized people in one of the most dangerous neighborhoods in the world. Through her ministry, thousands of people have been freed from drug addiction and have come to know Christ. Jackie has forsaken all personal safety and comfort to live in complete dependence on God. Her life is a testimony that true sacrifice for Christ is not always recognized by the world, but it has an eternal impact on the Kingdom of God.

Conclusion

Forsaking all for Christ is one of the most difficult demands of discipleship, but it is also one of the most rewarding. Throughout history, both the apostles and countless believers have demonstrated that the cost of following Christ is worth far more than anything the world can offer. The call to forsake the material, emotional, and spiritual for the Kingdom of God is a call to trust fully in the Lord and to live a life of radical obedience and sacrifice.

Though forsaking may seem painful or costly in the moment, the eternal rewards God has promised His followers far to outweigh any sacrifice we may make. The examples of the apostles and modern believers inspire us to live a life of total surrender to Christ, knowing that everything we forsake for His sake will be abundantly rewarded in the Kingdom of heaven. As disciples of Christ, we are called to follow His example, forsaking everything that hinders us from fulfilling our calling and trusting that He is faithful to provide and bless us beyond what we can imagine.

Chapter 11

Death to Self: Living for Christ

Introduction

The call of Christ to His disciples is not merely an invitation to follow Him but also a mandate to die to self. Jesus clearly stated in **Luke 9:23**, *"If anyone desires to come after Me, let him deny himself, and take up his cross daily, and follow Me."* This command to take up our cross daily signifies more than just facing hardships; it represents a daily death to our ambitions, desires, and will so that Christ can live in us. The apostle Paul expressed this principle in **Galatians 2:20**, *"I have been crucified with Christ; it is no longer I who live, but Christ lives in me."* Dying to self is an ongoing process that transforms our lives, frees us from selfishness, and leads us to live in full dependence on Christ.

Dying to self is not an empty sacrifice, but a pathway to a life filled with purpose, freedom, and fulfillment in Christ. The more we surrender our lives to Christ, the more we are filled with His presence and power. In this chapter, we will explore three key aspects of what it means to die to self and live for Christ: first, the transformation that occurs when we renounce our carnal desires; second, living according to the

Spirit versus living according to the flesh; and third, the ongoing process of dying to self to reflect the image of Christ.

The Transformation that Occurs When We Renounce Our Carnal Desires

Death to self begins with renouncing our carnal desires. In **Romans 8:13**, Paul writes, *"For if you live according to the flesh, you will die; but if by the Spirit you put to death the deeds of the body, you will live."* This verse emphasizes the importance of abandoning a life controlled by our impulses and carnal desires and, instead, living according to the Spirit. The flesh, which represents our sinful nature, constantly seeks to satisfy selfish desires and disobey God. However, by surrendering to Christ, we experience an internal transformation that frees us from the bondage of the flesh and empowers us to live a life of holiness and obedience.

This transformation does not happen automatically; it requires a conscious decision to submit to Christ daily. In **Ephesians 4:22-24**, Paul exhorts us to "put off your old self, which is being corrupted by its deceitful desires; to be made new in the attitude of your minds; and to put on the new self, created to be like God in true righteousness and holiness." The "old self" is our carnal nature, which must constantly be put off through the work of the Holy Spirit. When we renounce our carnal desires, we allow the "new self" in Christ to take control of our lives, resulting in a visible transformation in our character, attitudes, and actions.

The process of dying to self also involves a constant battle against the desires of the flesh. In **Galatians 5:17**, we are told that *"the flesh desires what is contrary to the Spirit,* *and the Spirit what is contrary to the flesh."* This struggle is part of the Christian life, but the good news is that through the Holy Spirit, we have the power to overcome the flesh. By relying on the Spirit, we experience the freedom to live in obedience to God rather than being enslaved to our carnal impulses. Transformation occurs when we allow the Spirit to guide our decisions and actions rather than giving in to the desires of the flesh.

Dying to self also means renouncing the pursuit of self-exaltation. In **Philippians 2:3**, Paul exhorts us, *"Do nothing out of selfish ambition or vain conceit. Rather, in humility value others above yourselves."* The flesh drives us to seek recognition and personal glory, but Christ calls us to live in humility and service to others. When we renounce the need for self-exaltation, we open the door for God to be exalted in our lives. This is the true transformation that occurs when we die to self: we stop seeking our own glory and begin living for the glory of God.

Additionally, dying to self leads us to relinquish control over our own lives. In **Proverbs 3:5-6**, we are told, *"Trust in the Lord with all your heart, and lean not on your own understanding; in all your ways acknowledge Him, and He shall direct your paths."* Selfishness drives us to want to control our circumstances and decisions, but dying to self means trusting in God's direction and yielding total control of our lives to Him. This surrender is not a sign of weakness but of complete trust in God's wisdom and plan for our lives.

Finally, the transformation that occurs when we die to self is manifested in a life of selfless service. In **Matthew 20:28**, Jesus said, *"The Son of Man did not come to be* *served, but to serve, and to give His life as a ransom for many."* When we follow Jesus' example and die to our own desires, we find the freedom to serve others with love and humility. This transformation allows us to reflect the character of Christ in our relationships and actions, showing the world what it truly means to live for Christ.

Living According to the Spirit vs. Living According to the Flesh

One of the keys to understanding what it means to die to self is recognizing the difference between living according to the Spirit and living according to the flesh. In **Romans 8:5-6**, Paul tells us, *"For those who live according to the flesh set their minds on the things of the flesh, but those who live according to the Spirit, the things of the Spirit. For to be carnally minded is death, but to be spiritually minded is life and peace."* This passage shows that living according to the flesh leads to spiritual death, while living according to the Spirit brings life and peace. Life according to the flesh is centered on selfish and temporary desires, while life according to the Spirit is focused on eternal matters and pleasing God.

Living according to the Spirit is not something we can achieve by our own strength; it is a fruit of the Holy Spirit's work in our lives. In **Galatians 5:16**, we are exhorted to *"walk by the Spirit, and you will not gratify the desires of the flesh."* This means that we must rely on the Holy Spirit to guide our decisions, thoughts, and actions. When we live according to the Spirit, we experience an internal transformation that enables us to overcome the flesh and live in obedience to God. This life according to the Spirit gives us the strength to say "no" to carnal desires and "yes" to God's will.

One of the most notable differences between life according to the flesh and life according to the Spirit is the fruit they produce. In **Galatians 5:19-21**, Paul describes the works of the flesh, which include *"sexual immorality, impurity, debauchery, idolatry, witchcraft, hatred, discord, jealousy, fits of rage, selfish ambition, dissensions, factions, envy, drunkenness, orgies, and the like."* These works of the flesh are the result of living a life controlled by selfish and sinful desires. In contrast, the fruit of the Spirit, described in Galatians 5:22-23, includes *"love, joy, peace, forbearance, kindness, goodness, faithfulness, gentleness, and self-control."* These fruits are the result of a life surrendered to the Spirit and reflect the character of Christ in us.

Another important distinction is that living according to the Spirit brings greater communion with God, while living according to the flesh drives us away from Him. In **Romans 8:8**, we are told that *"those who are in the flesh cannot please God."* The flesh is at enmity with God and will always seek to rebel against His will. However, when we live according to the Spirit, we enter into a deeper relationship with God because we are aligned with His will. This communion with God fills us with peace, joy, and purpose, while life according to the flesh only brings emptiness and destruction.

Living according to the Spirit also involves a renewed mind. **In Romans 12:2**, Paul exhorts us, *"Do not conform to the pattern of this world, but be transformed by the renewing of your mind."* Life according to the flesh conforms to the values and desires of the world, while life according to the

Spirit is aligned with God's thoughts and purposes. When we allow the Spirit to renew our minds, we are transformed and empowered to discern God's will for our lives. This renewal of the mind enables us to see the world from God's perspective and live according to His principles.

Finally, living according to the Spirit leads to a life of freedom. In **Galatians 5:1**, we are told, *"It is for freedom that Christ has set us free."* Life according to the flesh enslaves us because it is controlled by selfish and sinful desires. However, life according to the Spirit frees us to live in obedience to God and to fulfill His purpose for our lives. This freedom is not a license to sin but a freedom to live according to God's will, free from the condemnation and power of sin.

The Ongoing Process of Dying to Self to Reflect the Image of Christ

Dying to self is not a one-time event but a continuous process that lasts a lifetime. In **1 Corinthians 15:31**, Paul said, *"I die daily."* This testimony shows that dying to self is a daily act of surrender to Christ. Each day we face the temptation to live for ourselves, but we are called to deny ourselves, take up our cross, and follow Christ. This process of dying to self is painful, but it is necessary for Christ to live fully in us and for His image to be reflected through our lives.

The process of dying to self also involves total dependence on the Holy Spirit. In **2 Corinthians 3:18**, Paul tells us that *"we all, who with unveiled faces contemplate the Lord's glory, are being transformed into his image with ever-increasing glory, which comes from the Lord, who is the Spirit."* This transformation into the image of Christ is not something we can achieve by our own efforts; it is the work of the Holy Spirit in us. As we surrender to His work in our lives, the Spirit transforms us from the inside out, making us more like Christ.

This process of dying to self also leads us to greater humility. In **Philippians 2:5-8**, Paul exhorts us to have the same attitude that Christ had, who *"made himself nothing by taking the very nature of a servant."* Death to self involves stripping away our pride, ego, and personal ambitions. Like Christ, we are called to humble ourselves and serve others, placing their needs above our own. This act of humility reflects the character of Christ and is one of the clearest marks of a true disciple.

Furthermore, dying to self leads us to a life of sacrifice. In **Romans 12:1**, we are exhorted to *"present your bodies as a living sacrifice, holy and pleasing to God."* The Christian life is not about seeking our own comfort or personal satisfaction but about offering our lives as a sacrifice to God. This sacrifice involves giving up our desires, ambitions, and time for the sake of God's Kingdom. Although sacrifice is costly, it is through it that we experience the fullness of life in Christ.

Dying to self also leads us to a life of total dependence on God. In **John 15:5**, Jesus said, *"I am the vine; you are the branches. If you remain in me and I in you, you will bear much fruit; apart from me you can do nothing."* Death to self involves acknowledging our complete dependence on Christ. Without Him, we cannot live the Christian life or bear spiritual fruit. This acknowledgment leads us to deeper communion with God and a life of constant prayer, seeking His guidance and direction in every area of our lives.

Finally, the process of dying to self prepares us for eternal glory. In **2 Corinthians 4:16-17**, Paul wrote, *"Therefore we do not lose heart. Though outwardly we are wasting away, yet inwardly we are being renewed day by day. For our light and momentary troubles are achieving for us an eternal glory that far outweighs them all."* Death to self is not in vain; it is producing in us an eternal glory that will far surpass any sacrifice we make in this life. The more we die to ourselves, the more we prepare to experience God's glory in eternity.

In conclusion: Dying to self is one of the greatest challenges of Christian discipleship, but it is also one of the most transformative. Through this process, we are freed from carnal desires, renewed by the Holy Spirit, and transformed into the image of Christ. While dying to self involves sacrifice, suffering, and renunciation, it also brings a life of freedom, fulfillment, and communion with God. As we surrender our lives to Christ, we discover the true purpose of our existence: to live for His glory and to reflect His love and character to the world.

As disciples of Christ, we are called to die to self every day, trusting that God is working in us to make us more like His Son. Though this process is continuous and sometimes painful, the eternal rewards that await us far outweigh any temporary sacrifice. Dying to self is the key to experiencing the abundant life that Christ has promised us and to living in the power and fullness of the Holy Spirit.

Chapter 12

The Call of Today: A Challenge to the Modern Church

Introduction

Today, the church faces a significant challenge: to maintain purity and commitment to the radical call of following Christ in a world that constantly dilutes the message of the Gospel. Many modern churches have softened the cost of discipleship, presenting a faith that requires neither sacrifice nor surrender. However, Christ's call remains the same: to deny oneself, carry the cross, and follow Him. In a context where comfort, success, and self-exaltation are highly valued, the message of sacrifice and total surrender is more relevant than ever. The church needs an awakening that will bring it back to the foundational teachings of Jesus.

This chapter will address three crucial aspects for the modern church: first, the need to reclaim the true meaning of discipleship, which includes sacrifice and surrender; second, the danger of diluting the message of the Gospel to attract the world; and third, the challenge of living a more radical and committed faith that reflects the true cost of following Christ. These principles are essential not only for spiritual growth but also to impact the world with a Gospel that transforms lives from the inside out.

Diego Colón Batiz

The True Meaning of Discipleship: Sacrifice and Surrender

Discipleship according to Jesus is not an invitation to an easy or comfortable life, but a call to radical sacrifice. In **Luke 14:33**, Jesus said, *"So likewise, whoever of you does not forsake all that he has cannot be My disciple."* This passage reminds us that the cost of following Christ is high, and those who desire to be His disciples must be willing to sacrifice everything they have for Him. Throughout the Gospels, we see how Jesus continually challenged His followers to consider the cost of discipleship, which includes leaving behind possessions, relationships, and even their own lives. True discipleship involves complete surrender.

In contrast, many modern churches have presented a version of Christianity that demands neither surrender nor sacrifice. A faith centered on personal blessing, well-being, and prosperity has been promoted, where the cost of discipleship is often overlooked or minimized. This approach distorts Jesus' message, who never promised a life of comfort but rather a life marked by total submission to God's will. The challenge for the modern church is to remember that discipleship is not just about receiving but also about giving, and that following Christ implies sacrifice in every aspect of our lives.

Sacrifice is not limited to material possessions but includes the surrender of our will and personal desires. In Mark 8:34, Jesus said, "Whoever desires to come after Me, let him deny himself, and take up his cross, and follow Me." This call to self-denial is perhaps the most difficult aspect of discipleship, as it goes against human nature. The modern world encourages self-exaltation, personal fulfillment, and independence, but Christ's call is to die to self and follow Him, even when it means losing everything we consider valuable in this life.

Moreover, true discipleship involves being willing to suffer for Christ. In **2 Timothy 3:12**, Paul warns, ***"Yes, and all who desire to live godly in Christ Jesus will suffer persecution."*** Suffering is an inevitable part of following Christ because the Gospel challenges the world's systems and faces opposition. However, suffering for Christ is not in vain, as it produces deeper character and a stronger faith. The problem is that many Christians today seek to avoid suffering at all costs, preferring a Christianity that demands no sacrifice, but true discipleship cannot exist without this willingness to suffer.

The example of the first disciples, who left everything to follow Jesus, should serve as an inspiration for the modern church. These men and women gave up their jobs, their families, and their personal dreams to dedicate themselves completely to the mission of Christ. In a world where security and personal success are highly valued, the example of the apostles and other disciples who left everything to follow Jesus is a reminder that Christ's call always demands sacrifice and surrender. True discipleship involves a total and unconditional commitment.

Finally, true discipleship leads us to live for others. Jesus taught that the greatest in the Kingdom of Heaven is the one who serves others (**Matthew 23:11**). The modern church needs to recover this teaching and remember that following

Christ is not just about what we can receive, but also what we can give. Discipleships call us to a life of service, sacrificing our time, resources, and energy for the good of others. This is the essence of Christ's call, and only when the church once again embraces sacrifice, and surrender can it powerfully impact the world.

The Danger of Diluting the Message of the Gospel

One of the greatest dangers facing the modern church is the temptation to dilute the message of the Gospel to make it more attractive to the world. In an effort to attract the masses, many churches have softened the cost of discipleship and adopted a message that focuses more on self-help and prosperity than on the radical call of Jesus. This trend has led to a version of Christianity that is more centered on man than on God, where comfort and personal success are prioritized over sacrifice and holiness.

The apostle Paul warned about this danger in **2 Timothy 4:3-4:** *"For the time will come when they will not endure sound doctrine, but according to their own desires, because they have itching ears, they will heap up for themselves teachers; and they will turn their ears away from the truth, and be turned aside to fables."* Today, we see how many have stopped preaching the cross and sacrifice, and instead have presented a Gospel that conforms to the desires of culture. However, diluting the message of the Gospel is dangerous because it loses its transforming power. The true Gospel challenges the sinner, calls for repentance, and demands a change of life.

Another danger of diluting the Gospel is that it creates a false sense of security in believers. When the Gospel is presented without the call to repentance, sacrifice, and total surrender, people believe they can follow Christ without making radical changes in their lives. This is dangerous not only for individuals but also for the church as a whole, as it creates a superficial Christianity with no deep roots. Jesus warned about this in the parable of the sower, where the seeds that fall on shallow ground cannot withstand trials and persecutions **(Matthew 13:5-6)**. A shallow faith cannot withstand the challenges of the Christian life.

The danger of diluting the Gospel also manifests in the lack of holiness in the church. When the call to holiness and obedience to God's commandments is softened, believers begin to live according to the world's standards rather than Christ's. **Hebrews 12:14** tells us, *"Pursue peace with all people, and holiness, without which no one will see the Lord."* The church cannot impact the world if it conforms to it. The power of the Gospel lies in its ability to transform lives, and that transformation only happens when the church preaches the full Gospel, undiluted, calling people to holiness.

Another problem that arises when the Gospel is diluted is the loss of missionary urgency. When the message of the Gospel focuses solely on personal blessing and well-being, Christians lose the sense of urgency to share the message of salvation with the world. Jesus' mandate in **Matthew 28:19-20** to make disciples of all nations requires sacrifice, courage, and total commitment to the Kingdom of God. However, a diluted Gospel that does not emphasize mission and sacrifice creates a church more focused on itself than on fulfilling the Great Commission.

Finally, diluting the Gospel weakens the church's testimony before the world. Jesus said in **Matthew 5:13-14** that the church is the *"salt of the earth" and the "light of the world,"* but when the Gospel is softened, the church loses its flavor and its ability to shine in the darkness. The world needs to see a church that preaches and lives the radical Gospel of Christ, not a version that conforms to the world's desires. Only when the church returns to preaching the full Gospel can it truly impact a society thirsty for truth and transformation.

The Challenge of Living a Radical and Committed Faith

The modern church is called to live a more radical and committed faith, reflecting the true cost of following Christ. In **Revelation 3:16**, Jesus warns the church of Laodicea: *"So then, because you are lukewarm, and neither cold nor hot, I will vomit you out of My mouth*." This warning is a wake-up call for the church today, which has often become lukewarm in its commitment to Christ. Living a radical faith does not just mean attending church or participating in religious activities, but a daily and total commitment to Christ in every area of life.

The challenge of living a radical faith begins with the willingness to obey God in everything, even when His will goes against our desires. In **Luke 9:23**, Jesus said, *"If anyone desires to come after Me, let him deny himself, and take up his cross daily, and follow Me."* The cross represents death to self and total surrender to God's will. A radical faith means letting go of our ambitions, dreams, and desires to follow

God's plan, even when that plan involves sacrifice, discomfort, and suffering.

Living a radical faith also means being willing to face persecution for the sake of Christ. In **John 15:18-19**, Jesus warned His disciples that the world would hate them for following Him. Throughout history, true disciples of Christ have been persecuted, and today, in many parts of the world, Christians face similar opposition. Although many in the modern church seek to avoid conflict and persecution, Christ's call is to be willing to suffer for His sake, knowing that the reward in the Kingdom of Heaven is far greater than any earthly suffering.

Another mark of a radical faith is the commitment to Christ's mission. In **Matthew 28:19-20**, Jesus gave His disciples the mandate to make disciples of all nations. A church committed to this mission cannot afford to be complacent or passive. Living a radical faith means being actively involved in sharing the Gospel, both locally and globally. This requires sacrifices of time, resources, and energy, but it is an essential part of Christ's call for every believer. Radical faith does not settle for attending church on Sundays but seeks to expand God's Kingdom every day.

Prayer is another key component of a radical faith. In **1 Thessalonians 5:17**, we are exhorted to *"pray without ceasing."* A life of constant prayer reflects total dependence on God and a passion for His will. The modern church needs to rediscover the power of prayer, not just as a ritual act, but as a way of life that connects us with the heart of God and empowers us to live according to His purpose. Great revivals in history have always begun with people committed to prayer, and the same will be true for the church today.

Finally, a radical and committed faith requires a life of holiness. In **1 Peter 1:15-16**, we are exhorted: ***"Be holy in all your conduct, because it is written, 'Be holy, for I am holy.'"*** Holiness is not an outdated concept; it is the standard of living that God requires of His people. Living in holiness means separating ourselves from sin and committing to God's ways. In a world that promotes sin and immorality, the church is called to be different, to live a life that reflects God's character in everything we do. Only a church that lives in holiness can truly impact the world.

Christ's call has not changed, and the modern church is challenged to reclaim the true meaning of discipleship, which includes sacrifice, surrender, and total commitment to God. In a world that seeks comfort and self-exaltation, the message of the cross remains a radical challenge that demands we die to ourselves and live for Christ. The temptation to dilute the Gospel is great, but the transforming power of Christ's message is only manifested when it is preached in its entirety, without compromise or concessions.

The church is called to live a radical faith, committed to Christ's call and focused on His mission. Only a church that is willing to sacrifice, suffer for the Gospel, and live in holiness can make a lasting impact on the world. The challenge for the modern church is to set aside lukewarmness and complacency and embrace Christ's call to total surrender. The cost is high, but the eternal rewards are incomparable. As disciples of Christ, we are called to count the cost and decide if we are willing to follow Him to the very end.

Epilogue

A Call to Total Surrender

Throughout this book, we have explored the true cost of Christ's call. The path of discipleship is neither easy nor comfortable, but it is the only path that leads to a life of eternal purpose. We live in a time when many seek a Christianity without sacrifice, a Gospel that does not challenge our desires or require us to change. However, the message of Jesus remains clear: if we want to follow Him, we must be willing to give up everything. Authentic discipleship requires total surrender.

The challenge is not small, but the reward is great. Jesus does not call us to a life of comfort; He calls us to a life of transformation. He does not want us to simply follow Him from a distance, but to live in an intimate and constant relationship with Him. To do this, we must be willing to give up anything that hinders us from following His will. In each chapter, we have seen how this surrender involves self-denial, a willingness to carry our cross, and an unshakable commitment to His mission.

It is natural that, when considering this call, doubts and fears may arise. The cost seems high, and indeed it is. But Jesus promises that whoever loses their life for His sake will find it (**Matthew 16:25**). This is a promise we must remember constantly. In God's Kingdom, what seems like loss is gain, and what seems like surrender is actually the path to a fuller, more abundant life. We are not called to live by the values of this world but to embrace an eternal reality that surpasses anything we could imagine.

The cost of discipleship also calls us to a life of faith. Following Jesus means walking by faith, trusting that His plan is better than ours, even when we do not always understand it. In this process, we learn to rely on His grace rather than our own strength. Living a life of obedience to Christ involves relinquishing control and fully surrendering to His direction. This is perhaps the most difficult lesson for many of us: letting go of our own agendas and allowing Him to guide every aspect of our lives.

Obedience, as we have seen, does not always make sense from an earthly perspective. It may lead us down paths of suffering and difficulty. But the lives of disciples, both in the Bible and in modern times, show us that the greatest acts of faith and sacrifice are rewarded with God's transforming presence. When we choose to follow Jesus, even when the path is hard, we discover that He is with us every step of the way, strengthening and guiding us.

In this life of total surrender, we also discover that true freedom is not found in doing what we want, but in doing what God wants. Jesus said that we would know the truth, and the truth would set us free **(John 8:32)**. This freedom is not a license to live as we please, but the ability to live according to God's perfect design for our lives. In obeying Him, we find that our chains fall away, and we begin to live in the freedom that only His truth can provide.

However, we must be vigilant against the distractions the world offers us. Comforts, material success, and even our own ambitions can become obstacles that prevent us from following Christ's call. That is why discipleship requires constant watchfulness. We must regularly examine our hearts and be willing to remove anything that pulls us away from our devotion to Christ. This process of purification is ongoing, and it is through it that we become more like our Lord.

Once again, this call is not just for a few, but for all who decide to follow Christ. Every believer, regardless of background, is called to live a life of total surrender. This includes both spiritual leaders and lay members of the church. Each of us has a role to play in God's Kingdom, and each of us is called to pay the price of that calling. It is not an easy cost, but it is one worth paying because the reward is a life of eternal purpose in God's presence.

As you reflect on what you've read in this book, I want to invite you to make a personal evaluation. Are there areas of your life that you have not yet fully surrendered to God? Are you willing to let go of your own dreams and plans to embrace Christ's call, even if it means sacrifice? These are difficult questions, but they are essential for spiritual growth. Only when we are willing to fully surrender can we experience the fullness of life that Christ offers us.

My prayer is that this book has been a tool to challenge you to make more radical decisions in your walk with God. It is not just about gaining more knowledge of what it means to be a disciple; it is about living it. Each day, we face the choice of following Christ or following our own desires. I encourage you to choose to follow Jesus every day, knowing that the cost of following Him is high, but the eternal rewards are immeasurable.

Ultimately, Christ's call is not just to be followers, but to be disciples. To be disciples means we are committed to Him in every area of our lives. It is a call to daily surrender, to a deep and constant relationship with our Savior. And it is in that relationship that we find the true meaning of our lives. As you face the cost of discipleship, may His Spirit fill you with the strength and courage needed to press on.

The cost of the call may seem overwhelming, but we never walk alone. Jesus has promised that He will be with us to the very end of the age (**Matthew 28:20**). With His presence, we can face any challenge, any sacrifice, and any trial, knowing that we are on the path He has laid out for us. May the Lord bless you on this journey of obedience, and may you discover the unshakable joy that can only be found in surrendering completely to Him.

Questions for Deeper Insight

This chapter is designed to guide readers toward a deeper reflection on the topics addressed in the book. The following questions invite you to meditate on your own walk with Christ, consider the cost of discipleship, and evaluate whether you are willing to pay the price to follow Jesus more closely. Take time to answer sincerely and seek the guidance of the Holy Spirit as you reflect on each area of your life.

Chapter 1: What Does the Call Mean?

1. How do you understand Christ's call in your life? Do you feel you have fully responded to that call, or are there areas where you are still resisting?
2. In your daily life, what signs remind you of the cost of following Christ?
3. Reflect on the difference between being called and being chosen. Do you feel that God has chosen you for something specific?

Chapter 2: Denying Yourself

1. What personal desires are the hardest for you to deny in order to follow Christ?
2. How do you think modern culture clashes with the principle of self-denial? How can you combat those influences in your daily life?

3. Think of a recent example where you had to deny yourself for the love of Christ. What did you learn from that experience?

Chapter 3: Carrying the Cross

1. What does it mean to you to carry your cross daily? How do you apply this to your everyday life?
2. What personal challenges do you face in trying to live a life of surrender and sacrifice?
3. Can you identify a situation where you experienced joy while carrying your cross for Christ?

Chapter 4: The Cost of Commitment

1. What have you sacrificed so far for your commitment to Christ? Do you feel there are more things that God is calling you to give up?
2. How do you handle the pressure of the world, which is often against the Christian principles you practice?
3. Reflect on a moment when you felt the cost of following Christ was too high. How did God help you overcome that feeling?

Chapter 5: The Sacrifice of Your Own Will

1. When was the last time you had to sacrifice your own will to follow God's will?
2. What areas of your life are you still trying to control instead of surrendering completely to God?

3. How can you imitate Jesus in His total submission to the Father's will, even when it is difficult?

Chapter 6: The Disciple's Spiritual Warfare

1. Do you recognize that you are in a daily spiritual battle? What are your biggest challenges in this fight?
2. What spiritual weapons are you using to resist the enemy? Is there one you could use more effectively?
3. How do you rely on God's armor during times of trial and temptation?

Chapter 7: The Reward of the Call

1. What spiritual rewards have you experienced by following Christ, despite the difficulties?
2. How have you seen joy and peace as the fruit of your obedience to God?
3. How do you maintain an eternal perspective in the midst of daily trials?

Chapter 8: The Call to Serve

1. In what ways are you serving others in the name of Christ? How can you improve in your service?
2. Reflect on Jesus as the perfect servant. What areas of your life require more humility to follow His example?
3. What sacrifices have you made to serve others, and how have you seen God work through them?

Chapter 9: Persecution and Rejection

1. Have you experienced persecution or rejection for following Christ? How did you handle those situations?
2. How do you remain faithful under the pressure of being accepted by today's culture?
3. How can you strengthen your faith to face potential persecutions in the future?

Chapter 10: Renouncing Everything

1. Is there something in your life that you feel God is calling you to give up, but you are still holding on to it?
2. Reflect on the concept of renouncing the material, emotional, and spiritual. What have you given up so far in following Christ?
3. What modern or biblical examples have inspired you to make greater sacrifices for the Kingdom?

Chapter 11: Death to Self

1. What does dying to "self" mean in your daily life? What aspects of your character need to be more submitted to Christ?
2. How can you live more according to the Spirit and less according to the flesh?
3. How can you better reflect Christ's image in your life through a continuous process of death to self?

Chapter 12: Today's Call

1. How does the cost of discipleship in modern culture personally challenge you?
2. Are there areas in your life where you feel you have diluted the message of the Gospel? How can you be firmer in proclaiming the full truth?
3. What concrete steps can you take to live a more radical and committed faith?

Conclusion of the Reflection Section

The key to each of these topics is action. God has called you to a life of obedience and sacrifice, but the eternal rewards and the fullness of living in His will far surpass anything the world can offer. These questions are just the beginning of a continuous process of surrender, reflection, and growth. Let the Holy Spirit guide you through each challenge you face, remembering that the cost of the call is high, but the rewards in Christ are infinite.

About the Author

Diego Colón Batiz is a passionate leader with nearly 30 years of ministry experience, dedicated to training leaders committed to God's call. He currently serves as the Director of the Department of Education for the Florida Church of God Hispanic Region, a role in which he oversees and develops programs focused on equipping ministers for effective service in God's Kingdom.

His ministry is characterized by a clear focus on teaching, mentoring, and equipping new leaders, helping them understand the demands and cost of the call. Diego has been an influential voice in training generations of workers, sharing from his personal experience the challenges and blessings of obeying God's call.

"The Cost of the Call" reflects his desire to help believers and leaders understand that following Christ involves sacrifice, obedience, and a radical commitment to

God's work. Through this book, he offers a unique perspective based on his ministerial journey and deep knowledge of Scripture.

Diego also deeply values spending time with his family, considering it a cornerstone of his life and ministry. In his free time, he enjoys worship and modeling a practical and genuine faith both at home and in the church, demonstrating that the call to serve begins in everyday life.